WITHDRAWN
Tavistock and Portman NHS Trust Library

TAVISTOCK LIBRARY
TAVISTOCK CENTRE
120 BELSIZE LANE
LONDON NW3 5BA

Tavistock and Portman Library
10032261

Classmark: QLJ JED LP
Acc. No: M3522

CHAIRING CHILD PROTECTION CONFERENCES

Chairing Child Protection Conferences

An exploration of attitudes and roles

ANN LEWIS
School of Social Work, University of East Anglia

Avebury
Aldershot • Brookfield USA • Hong Kong • Singapore • Sydney

© A. Lewis 1994

All rights reserved. No part of this publication may be reproduced, stored in a retrieval system, or transmitted in any form or by any means, electronic, mechanical, photocopying, recording or otherwise without the prior permission of the publisher.

Published by
Avebury
Ashgate Publishing Limited
Gower House
Croft Road
Aldershot
Hants GU11 3HR
England

Ashgate Publishing Company
Old Post Road
Brookfield
Vermont 05036
USA

Typeset by Neville Young
49 Muswell Avenue
London N10 2EH

British Library Cataloguing in Publication Data

Lewis, Ann
  Chairing Child Protection Conferences:
  Exploration of Attitudes and Roles
  I. Title
  362.768532

ISBN 1 85628 691 6

Library of Congress Cataloging-in-Publication Data

Lewis, Ann, 1936–
  Chairing child protection conferences : an exploration of attitudes and roles / Ann Lewis
    p. cm.
  Includes bibliographical references.
  ISBN 1-85628-691-6 : $55.95 (U.S. : est.)
  1. Social case work with children--Great Britain. 2. Social work administration--Great Britain. 3. Child welfare workers--Great Britain--Attitudes. I. Title
  HV751.A6L44   1994
  362.7'1--dc20
                                                                94-24837
                                                                    CIP

Printed and Bound in Great Britain by
Athenaeum Press Ltd, Newcastle upon Tyne.

Contents

Acknowledgements   vii

Introduction   viii

Part I

1   The history of child protection conferences   3

2   Dilemmas for chairs in holding child protection conferences   10

3   The task of conferences in child protection in relation to chairing   19

4   Chairing and small group dynamics   27

5   Decision-making and chairing   32

6   The techniques and skills of chairing   40

Part II

7   Methodological framework   51

8   Training   58

9   Preparation   61

10   Managing the conference   66

11	Style, power and status	78
12	The child and the parents	84
13	The chairs' attitudes to child abuse and neglect	90
14	Is there a 'better' case conference?	94

Part III

| 15 | An overview of chairing child protection conferences | 99 |

Appendix I	115
Appendix II – the guided interview schedule	118
Bibliography	120

Acknowledgements

My thanks are due to the 14 chairpersons in the study, for their time, their readiness and their frankness in discussing their thoughts about chairing with me.

Also to Professor Martin Davies and Dr June Thoburn of the University of East Anglia who have been so tolerant and encouraging but stringent about my efforts.

Brian Corby's thoughtful comments have been immensely helpful too as I redrafted the text.

And not least, thanks to many dear friends for their support and to Derek for providing daily backup at home.

Introduction

The skills of the chair are crucial. (Jean Moore, 1992)

An inevitable part of a practitioner's work in child care is to attend many case conferences. Over my own seventeen years as a practitioner it did not need great perception to notice how different were the styles of chairing, nor great acumen to know that some case conferences arrived at their decisions more quickly and competently than others and that coming away from some case conferences, they could be rated 'better' than others. Why should this be so?

It would be possible to ask questions of the chairs from the practical point of view about what methods they used to perform their task and from the theoretical point of view about what they thought they were doing.

It was obvious too that, apart from the technicalities of chairing conferences, that the chairs had to deal with a variety of views and opinions on childhood, parenting, abuse or neglect which might be expressed by any member of the conference. It was likely that there would be hidden agendas about members' own personal experiences of abuse, their inter agency differences and their beliefs about when an intervention was appropriate in family life. Part of the task for the chairperson was to take account of this range of views and value judgements. If the chairperson did not take charge, then almost certainly, a long and complicated conference would ensue. Had the chairs devised strategies for dealing with these other unspoken issues?

The ideas of neutrality and objectivity in relation to chairing were also interesting. If divisions emerged in conferences they would tend to be along agency lines with social workers being loyal to social workers and health visitors to health visitors and so on. A chairperson could be a line manager and closely involved in the casework aspects of cases, as well as the plans and decisions concerning the families so how did objectivity fare then?

There was an expectation that the chairperson would be neutral in the conference. How was it possible? Although objectivity about the alleged abuse was an aim, it was difficult to achieve, as was objectivity about the responses. It would be intriguing to explore how the people who chaired the conferences attempted to be neutral.

So in approaching the literature for this study, there were two distinct parts. One was the literature on parenting and child abuse and neglect and the other on the dynamics of case conferences and chairing skills. There was such an extensive literature in both these fields that it was necessary to abandon one in the interests of word length so reluctantly the sections on parenting and child abuse and neglect were excised! However there are many fascinating books available on these subjects and to read them is to gain in understanding about the chairing of child protection conferences. The complexities for the chairs in handling the interaction between such highly-charged subjects as bringing up children and the causes of abuse and neglect as well as the more mundane and pragmatic matters of running a meeting to achieve certain decisions, are multitudinous.

The fieldwork for the original thesis on which this book is based was started in the Autumn of 1990. It soon became apparent how rapidly the framework for child protection procedures was changing. These changes are set out in Appendix I and are important for understanding the setting in which the people who chaired the conferences were interviewed.

Part I

1 The history of child protection conferences

The crucible of the system. (Louis Blom-Cooper, 1987)

It seems worthwhile, when studying a particular activity, to trace its history and development for clues as to its present form. Case conferences are no exception to this. They have a varied and interesting history of their own and as a starting point, their history sets the scene for examining the chairing of conferences.

Case Conferences were the predecessors of Child Protection conferences and have been in existence for nearly 50 years. They appear to have had a chequered history in which the term has been used to cover a number of different functions.

A team conference

It is difficult to pin-point when case conferences were first used but the earliest reference found was in a text-book on Child Guidance from the 40s (Burbury, Balint and Yapp 1945). It indicates that the 'case conference' was in use as a team conference about a case. It was a conference to which other professionals were invited – teachers, probation officers, social workers and medical staff and was a forum for discussing a case before an audience interested in such work but not necessarily with responsibility for the case. Criticism and doubts were expressed about the meeting being open to public discussion but there was full advocacy for a conference being a team discussion because 'they are about the same purpose – to seek help for the child and family and they (the members of the team) trust each other' (p. 134).

The journal 'Case Conference' was first produced in 1954 suggesting that the term, being used as the title of the journal must have been in common usage and relevant to a wide range of social workers at that date. In the review of subscribers between 1954 and 1970, (when the journal became the professional publication of the British Association of Social Workers) the largest groups of subscribers at the beginning were Psychiatric Social Workers (16%) and Child Care officers (14%), lending a little weight to the guess that the term came from the psychiatric setting, in the first instance and was adapted over the years to the child care setting from Child Guidance.

A group discussion

Case conferences are mentioned in much of the literature of the 50s. A project on marital problems undertaken by the Family Discussion Bureau (Bannister et al 1955) comments 'The case conferences have remained throughout, the central feature of the project and have given a general sense of unity and direction to the work' (p. 13). They are 'neither committees which make decisions nor consultations with a teacher who gives direct guidance. They are group discussions in which the dynamics of the marriage and of the relationship between the client and the worker can be explored and clarified so that the worker can see for herself her next step in the case-work process' (p. 15). 'The case conference is never to give the worker definite instructions about her handling of the case. They rather provide for her an opportunity to learn from others' experience so that she can clarify and evaluate what is personal in her approach and proffer and test her own ideas about the case' (p. 14). This reference indicates that the case conference is exactly what it suggests at this stage – a conference about a case, but attended only by the professionals involved.

A description of case conferences being the place to absorb the feelings which professionals expressed as a result of their disappointment at not being able to help problem families, was found in the journal for the Family Welfare Association (1954). 'This is why any discussion on problem families and many a case conference called by the various social agencies who are interested in a particular family, so often turns from aiming to clarify the problem, to ways of drastically eradicating it – it is as though all the disappointment and frustration of the social agencies suddenly boils up and impatience and resentment hinders understanding and acceptance.'

This description suggests conferences were used by professionals to express their feelings about the cases which caused them anger and distress.

For co-ordination

References to case conferences in the social work texts of the early 60s are rare and even though their use was officially recommended by government guidelines as good practice (DHSS LASSL (74) 13 1974) they are surprisingly infrequent in the texts on child care and child abuse in the 70s. Olive

Stevenson (Social Review 1960) reviews co-ordination as an essential aspect of any professional meeting about a child, as exemplified by a Co-ordinating Committee at work. She picks out how the differing views of the different professionals can create a potential of collusion or conflict. She advocates 'preserving a healthy tension' (p. 115) despite what she sees as a difference of function and involvement by the field workers from different professions. Arriving with different social philosophies and with different skills arising from their own professional training they therefore give priority to different problems. She brings into view for the first time the problem of power and sectional loyalties when representatives from the higher levels of organisations meet, and she recommends with great clarity and foresight that there are two requirements for co-ordination – deeper personal insight and a wider vision of the objectives of the social services as a whole. The Co-ordinating Committees of the 1950s appear to have handed co-ordination to case conferences.

Co-ordinating Committees were recommended in 1950 by the Ministries of Education and Health and the Home Office. Local authorities had to establish them to consider plans for families who neglected their children but it seems that the frequency and use of these meetings was limited and depended on whether the professionals concerned initiated them. They were certainly widespread but used more as general meetings of the higher status local professionals as case discussions and not so much for the workers in the field.

Views about the usefulness of case conferences varied. Elizabeth Irvine (in Younghusband 1965) hints that such meetings are a good idea when she describes the plight of the children of mothers admitted to mental hospital. 'Child Care officers, probation officers, and health visitors all have contact with these families and the help they offer can be tremendously increased by communication and co-operation with those treating the patient. It is vital that there should be some machinery for ensuring that somebody is available and sensitive to the needs of every family exposed to such stress – or at least every family containing children ...' This reference suggests the idea of a key worker role.

In 1970 the Department of Health and Social Security sent a circular to the Medical Officers and the Children's Officers of local authorities bringing to their attention the problem that young children were being injured by their parents (p. 30 Auckland Inquiry Report 1975). They were asked to arrange local discussions of the problem, bringing together GPs, Paediatricians, Accident and Emergency consultants, police, NSPCC representatives and other local people. Such groups were to have a continuing function with the Co-ordinating Committees, which passed from the Medical Officer of Health to the Divisional Social Services District Officer in 1971. They were to 'consider children neglected in their own homes.' In the case of Susan Auckland, the third child of three children all under 2½ years, born to parents who could not cope and where the first child had been killed by her father, one of the reasons cited for her death was the lack of a Co-ordinating Committee to address her individual needs.

For collaboration

By 1969, Richardson (in M.L.Kellmer Pringle 1969) describes a case conference as a method of teaching professionals how to work together. He offered six professional and amateur social workers a complex family case history. 'After two hours of sometimes rather warm discussion, they evolved the semblance of a co-operative multi-pronged attack consisting of several phases, and, to my surprise and pleasure, they agreed on a co-ordinator for the plan.' (p. 18) But Mary Evans dismisses case conferences with 'all that has really occurred is that professionals have gone away thinking how co-operative they are' (p. 63). However Joan Cooper recommends them. 'The practice of having regular case conferences and reviews about families bringing together senior and junior residential staff as well as senior and other child care officers seems an admirable way of ensuring that consultation takes place.' (p. 88)

The Tunbridge Wells Study Group document on Non-Accidental Injury to Children circulated by the Department of Health and Social Security in 1973 and 1974 for 'the information of Local Authorities and Executive Councils' and published in 1975 as an edited book, proved to be an important turning point because it gathered together inter-professional views about the management of child abuse and in an appendix on the case conference specifically advocated its use because it could be the arena for collaboration. It was to bring together all the available information, all who made decisions, and all who provided services. One key person might co-ordinate treatment but the case conference was to retain responsibility for each step. They too pointed to the importance of each professional member of the team retaining their professional role – the doctor to save life; the social services to protect through its statutory duty and the police to detect crime and maintain the law. 'Case conferences and full communication will help to develop mutual trust and increase the value of the contribution made to the family.' (p. 27) The importance of professional trust re-emerges as an essential ingredient in multi-disciplinary understanding and working together. Collaboration moves joint working to a higher level than coordination because of the trust engendered when professionals work closely together. Coordination prevents the professionals from standing on one another's toes on the family's door-step. Collaboration enables them to enter the family home together with some confidence about how to carry out the task in hand cooperatively.

For the management of child abuse

By the mid-1970s case conferences were established and recognised as the arena in which the problems of injured or at risk children would be managed but not until 1976 were the police given guidelines about being involved. A senior police officer was to be included in all case conferences and relevant information about previous convictions in a family was to be made available to the case conference. Prevention, prediction and early identification were meant to be enhanced by the procedures though this aim was queried in its practice by Parton (p. 131). He estimated that the case conferences presented a serious threat to civil liberties because of the absence of parents and children and that it was only a 'private professional organisational arena' (p. 197).

The Inquiry reports into the deaths of Maria Colwell and Susan Auckland (1974 and 1975) both noted the absence of case conferences at key moments in their histories and criticised the lack of communication and liaison between the professionals.

The reports on Malcolm Page (1981) and Maria Mehmedagi (1987) made specific comments on case conferences:

a case conference should be called within a short period of the first major incident

knowledge of the family should be shared

a diagnosis of the problem should be made as well as the *degree* of risk of abuse

a key-worker should be allocated

a treatment plan should be drawn up and a procedure for monitoring established

registration should be decided on and whether to inform parents.

'We consider that in cases of child abuse the case conference should define in its recommendations what are the standards below which a family should not be allowed to fall before remedial action is taken.' (p. 59) This list begins to give shape to the kind of conferences described by the chairs interviewed for this study.

The report on Jasmine Beckford (1985) ranges widely in its comments about abuse, case conferences and social work practice. Blom-Cooper highlighted the lessons from the Maria Colwell case as: decision-making, risk-taking and policing/surveillance. He recommended that chairs consider whether a child should be involved and he emphasised the importance of objectivity. 'The over-riding consideration of case conferences is that they should inject into the process of decision-making an objectivity that cannot be obtained by those directly involved in the management of a child abuse case.' (p. 250) He was critical of case conferences for being indecisive and of chairing practices.

In his report on Kimberley Carlile (1987) he set out again a wide context referring to the long history of abusive parent/child relationships in society; to child homicide figures; to predisposing factors in child abuse but also noting that 'Social Services Departments are protecting nearly 30,000 children who have been determined at multi-disciplinary case conferences and in court hearings to have been seriously injured or who are at serious risk of injury' focusing on a greater importance for the case conference. He referred to it as the 'crucible of the system' for the future. All of the child death inquiry reports in the 80s criticised the lack of communication between the agencies as a causative factor in the tragedies (p. 60 Reder et al 1993) and as a result a great deal of effort was concentrated into improving the structures of child protection and their management. In the event, this did not prevent further mismanagement of complex situations. (Orkney Report 1991)

For the protection of the child

Also in the 80s case conferences are constantly mentioned in the social work texts and they were developed in the context of child protection. The two strands leading to their current form appear to stem from the psychiatric hospital setting and from the child guidance setting. In both settings, multi-disciplinary meetings planned therapeutic strategies for patients or co-ordinated interventions for disadvantaged families. They gave priority to professionals working together. However, it is only since Working Together (1988) that the protection of the child has assumed priority as the main purpose of the conference. It is as recently as Working Together (1991) that the name has changed to the child protection conference.

During the months before the crisis in Cleveland, 175 case conferences were held and parents were not involved in any of them. 'During the crisis parents felt a strong sense of grievance that conference members were making recommendations and decisions about them and their children without, as they saw it, their views being heard.' (Cleveland Report 1988, p. 58) This call for parents' views to be heard, expressed publicly what had been expressed privately by many parents and some social workers for a number of years about the injustice of a system which precluded parents from taking part in conferences. The presence of parents and children as an integral part of the child protection conference occurred at the same time as the change in name, and expresses the change in nature of the child protection conference from the nature of the case conference in the past. The case for parental participation is made elsewhere (Thoburn at al, forthcoming) but parents' involvement in the child protection process requires a different type of chairing in conferences. The child protection conference becomes a different meeting when parents and children are present. Professionals may no longer speculate about a family. They are expected to present information and evidence which must be substantiated in the meeting. The family need preparation and should be enabled to say what they wish to say in the meeting. As Department of Health figures suggest (1989) over 70 per cent of the children who are conferenced, remain at home with their parents, so it makes good sense that they should be the key people to protect their children and therefore should be involved in the decision-making. The conference is better approached as a business meeting and conducted formally with an agenda. This has involved a major shift for the chairperson and other professionals to adapt to, especially without benefit of training. Discussing the protection of the child in the presence of parents has become a highly skilled task for a chairperson to deal with.

Summary

In this chapter, an attempt has been made to describe the strands of historically different meetings which have united to become the present child protection conferences. The chairs of case conferences in the past were dealing with a very different meeting from the new child protection conferences. They used to be more informal, more relaxed and rather unstructured occasions. An analysis therefore, of their chairing style was not so vital. The chairs' role in child protection procedures has changed to that of key actor. Much depends on the quality of chairing especially since family members may be present. The Children Act 1989 ushered in the era of participation and partnership and the public role of the chairperson is to be seen as a symbol or model of those principles.

2 Dilemmas for chairs in holding child protection conferences

> *Their [social workers'] task is to calculate the risks involved for children in each situation ... and balance this against what seems fair to parents. They must do this in the light of legal rules, community values and resource factors.*
> (Brian Corby, 1993)

There are a number of ethical dilemmas for chairs in holding conferences. This chapter will explore some of them.

Stepping over the boundary of family life

When a chairperson carries out the task of chairing a child protection conference s/he embarks on a process of decision-making which may lead to major changes in the life of the family and of the individual child, frequently without their permission. Here the state steps over the boundary into private family life even though government guidelines are at pains to stress that the conference has no legal powers. Before child protection procedures were in existence such decisions were taken by the Court only.

In case conferences and later in child protection conferences, it was custom and practice, for discussions to take place and usually for decisions to be made about the likely risk to the child, without the family being aware of them and certainly, for the most part, without the family being present. This situation is swiftly changing as parents are increasingly attending conferences and taking part in the discussion and decision-making. Whereas, in the past, social work intervention took place either with parental consent, albeit reluctantly at times, or by order of the Court, current child protection intervention can take place without consent as a result of an allegation of abuse or neglect from any source or as a result of a conference decision made after investigation.

As with the social work issue of when to use care and when to use control, a similar dilemma exists for social workers and the chairs of conferences about initiating intervention in private family life in child protection. Questions arise about whether it can be justified in terms of the social work relationship, especially when the family might be unaware of the allegations and might not be allowed to be present at the meeting where the incident or neglect is discussed.

An Area Director in E. Sussex at the time of the Colwell case said of the public criticisms of the social worker following the tragic death of the child, 'It felt so totally unreasonable, so totally unjust ... so sensational, which was beyond our experience because until that time nothing had been more private than social work.' Hutchinson comments (1986), 'until then they (social workers) had regarded their work as private between themselves and their clients.' Child protection procedures after this time, increasingly became the authority for intervention by social workers into family life. The case conference became the arena where the family's private behaviour was tested publicly by the professionals.

Blom-Cooper attempted to hold such interventions in a balance by saying, on the one hand, 'We would have fewer failures if society supported greater intervention from the welfare agencies' (Beckford Report p. 136) and on the other, 'Society, rightly in our opinion, is not prepared to tolerate too heavy-handed disruptions to family life and expects careful judgement to be exercised in deciding on the appropriate action to be taken in any particular case. This more flexible approach offers some security to families.' (p. 136)

Family case-work used to be the basic tool of social work because it 'developed personality through adjustments consciously effected, individual by individual between men and their social environment' (Mary Richmond 1954) and because it helped social workers 'concentrate on the problems of helping individuals to use existing services and to marshal their outer and inner resources.' This intensely private model of working, using family case-work, gave way to a much more public model of social work because of the child protection procedures. The issue of intervention and especially of investigation into abuse or neglect is highlighted in child protection procedures. The chairperson of a conference is placed directly in that dilemma of whether to step over the boundary of family life in a public way.

Making an intervention

White Franklin posed a question in 1975 (p. 168) about 'whether and how far the problems raised by NAI to children within the family are accepted as community problems and always to be settled by team decision and action?'. Since then the case conference appears to have taken on the role of the decision-making authority for agreed interventions and the chairperson is responsible for ensuring that a decision is reached about such intervention.

John Stroud's comment (White Franklin 1975 p. 102) that 'the removal of the child from the family circle needs stronger justification than protecting him within it' and that the case conference should 'lean towards positive action to help the family', suggests that interventions were seen at that time in the helping context.

Dingwall, Eekalaar and Murray (1983) recognise a stage of intervention by the child protection procedures which should be carried out before compulsory intervention is required. They suggest the procedures should monitor when two events occur: 'parental incorrigibility (parents fail to co-operate) and failure of containment (concern moves beyond the small group of front-line workers – skills are exhausted).' They indicate that a degree of severity regarding the abuse or neglect needs to have been reached before compulsory intervention takes place and they imply an expectation that the conference should initiate and complete some of this work before that stage is reached.

Corby and Mills (1986 p. 531-542) argue for minimum intervention as long as the protection of the child is assured. 'This can only be achieved if the system designed and those operating it function in a purposeful and clearly thought-out manner. The hub of the child abuse system is the case conference attended by all involved professionals.' (p. 532) Their findings led them to be critical of the conferences because of the lack of adequate risk analysis and of appropriate resources to help families.

A more highly-charged view of social work intervention in child protection in the 1980s was that it was deemed to be 'ideally about danger, seriousness and proper assessment of risk' but was more likely to be 'about fears of acting alone, lack of professional judgment and pressure of work' (Dale et al 1986). Before this the 'rule of optimism' (Dingwall, et al 1983) was described and criticised as dangerous. It was a model of thinking in which professionals tended to describe parental behaviour in optimistic terms as 'cultural relativism' or as assumptions of natural love which were used as an excuse for parental deviance. Both these views were unhelpful to families and professionals alike. Later, looking back on the '80s, (Community Care 1991) Dale describes a 'rule of pessimism' as the more likely professional approach which followed. He says professionals viewed 'clients and families as inherently bad, deceptive, and constitutionally (as opposed to situationally) violent or perverse.' In this sort of context 'a siege mentality can arise where staff may ultimately come to feel persecuted by clients.' In his view 'prospects of positive change tended to be viewed with scepticism and manifestations of such, as client manipulation.' He added to this criticism the view that current interventions using assessment over a longer-term time-scale and influenced more by 'humanistic therapeutic principles (which do not exclude appropriate challenging) than by earlier confrontational models' is preferable because he thinks it offers parents an opportunity to work in partnership as well as enabling clear decisions to be reached about long-term case management.

Cooper and Ball (1987) use Whittaker and Garbarino's four systems within the environment to illustrate the way child protection interventions take place. The micro-system represents the family's close day-by-day relationships. The meso-system links and relates the micro-systems of the family and the social worker. They may function both separately and together in general child care. The exo-system represents someone else's system over which the individual may have no control and where the child protection procedures may be located. Beyond these there is the macro-system which is the broadest, ideological, political pattern of a culture. It includes society's views about the value of children and the quality of parent-child relationships and the phenomenon of child abuse.

Cooper and Ball describe the case conference as part of the exo-system which 'most menaces abusing parents in the way it makes recommendations which are then implemented by the social worker who is part of the micro-system.' In their terms the conference prescribes both the social work and the expected response from the family without necessarily the consent of either and without the family seeing the conference (the exo-system) as a working reality.

These criticisms about a lack of a clearly prescribed focus for conferences and the spot-lighting of the importance of making appropriate plans for working with families, illustrate the dilemma for the chairs about intervention. They are expected to call the conference in time to prevent further abuse or neglect and yet, they should not call the conference too soon because there is an expectation that some work should be carried out first. Achieving the balance is crucial for future work with the family because the system may otherwise effectively threaten rather than help the parents and the child.

The visibility of child abuse

A further problem for chairs to bear in mind when holding child protection conferences is the likelihood that the families will be socially disadvantaged. The following quotation was written in 1954: 'Insufficient income, overdrawn budget, rent arrears, pawning, chronic illness and under-nourishment, mental deficiency, mental illness, unemployment.' (Margaret Whale 1954) Despite the fact that it is nearly 40 years old, apart from substituting credit cards and finance companies for 'pawning', the description could easily fit many families who currently come within the child protection procedures. A checklist of observations used by the NSPCC in their assessments of families referred because of allegations of abuse or neglect (Gilmour 1988) mirrors exactly Margaret Whale's descriptions. She also points to the 'strain and stress between the family and the community.' These are the signals from families referred for child abuse or neglect but where the procedures may be invoked too readily simply because the families are already known to the welfare agencies.

Parton (1985) argues strongly that child abuse is not 'like a disease which requires prevention, identification and treatment' but 'serious attention must be given to the social structural factors involved' (p. 172). His sources are mainly American but he believes the situation to be similar in Britain. He quotes Pelton's discussion of the 'myth of classlessness' in which he points out that the available statistics lead to the conclusion that the lower socio-economic classes are disproportionately represented among cases known to the public agencies because 'poor people are more available to public scrutiny, and likely to be known to social agencies and law enforcement agencies whose workers have had the opportunity to enter their households'. He shows that poverty, social deprivation and economic disadvantage are factors influencing the quality of child care standards in families because of the stresses they entail and he is in favour of professionals alleviating the resultant suffering rather than identifying child abuse as a symptom to be treated in families already known to the welfare agencies.

Moral issues

The literature on the history of childhood (Aries 1972, De Mause 1976, Hardyment 1983, Gathorne-Hardy 1972, Kevill-Davies 1991, Pollock 1983, Stainton Rogers 1992) shows how appallingly children have suffered over the centuries because of adult cruelty and neglect but nevertheless it is a shock to discover that a child said in 1988 'It's my job to suffer', in reference to the abuse she was experiencing (Gilmour 1988). The moral justification for society intervening on behalf of the child in instances like this one, is undeniable. The child is vulnerable and in need of protection.

In the past, professionals were able to justify holding a case conference because it was about helping the family. Improving the social worker's understanding of the psycho-dynamics of the situation and then improving the service to the family by co-ordinating the efforts of the professionals, underpinned their action. Nowadays the justification would be described as the need to protect the child, yet this has led professionals into secretiveness and exclusivity in the recent past and sometimes causing more harm than good in their attempts to protect the child. The people who chair conferences have been placed in a moral dilemma about making decisions behind closed doors. Benn pleads (Benn and Gans 1983) that 'all morality must be in principle public: it cannot have the private standing of "gut feelings", immediate, incommunicable as reasons, invoked at best to explain actions but unable to justify them except to someone else who happens to share those feelings.' One of the problems of the case conference was that it contained many 'gut feelings' expressed by professionals without the constraints of the 'public principle' and conferences have sometimes been guilty of making decisions and interventions on that basis. The presence of parents counteracts that tendency. The absence of parents in conferences in the past, may be criticised as a moral gap. With the increasing practice of inviting parents to conferences the gap should close. 'Inasmuch as we can and do discuss what is the right thing to do, we think the moral judgments and decisions as capable of being supported and defended by reasons good for anyone, which any normally rational person would recognise.' The presence of parents requires conference members to be open and honest in a way which was not previously required. Benn argues for a liberal moral theory in which states and their agents are licensed to set aside moral principles when necessary, for the sake of good outcomes (or to avoid bad ones) and that the reason for this is that they are 'the champions and trustees of the public in a jungle world'. The child protection conference is referred to in the literature as 'the hub', 'the arena', 'the crucible' of the child protection procedures and as such is the place where the protection of the child is given priority. The Beckford Report stated that the agencies must act as the champion or trustee for the child. An incident of alleged harm to one being by another is regarded in a liberal moral theory as an act in which the state can properly interfere through the criminal law. 'No-one has a right to be unselfish with other people's interests.' (p. 155 Hugh Cecil cited in Benn)

The state may choose to be paternalistic in its other interventions, for example with regard to seat belts and crash helmets imposing safety on its citizens. There are, however, two questions which require answering in these situations. Firstly, 'Does the public have a reason to interfere?' and secondly, 'Does it have the right to interfere?'. Insofar as child abuse and neglect are concerned these two moral questions are implicit in the holding of a conference. The chairperson of a conference must surely ask such questions of her/himself and the other professionals involved.

A feminist critique of the public/private dichotomy and the family/state dilemma (Carole Pateman in 'Public and Private in Social Life') calls for an extension of the liberal moral principles to women as well as men and for domestic life to be acknowledged as being at the heart of civil society rather than apart or separate from it. Experience has shown that for 'families' read 'mothers and children' especially among client families. Patriarchal structures have supported interventions and legislation which have subordinated women and children in the past but women's rights and children's rights are rising in the public's awareness and the child protection conference is one arena where they are meant to have full recognition. In child protection, women and children need extra support in terms of finance and resources, to promote good outcomes for them, rather than inquisitorial and adversarial interventions.

In the field of child abuse or neglect the child protection conference is the place where the moral issues of openness and fairness should be acted out. Holding the conference should be as a result of those values being debated by the chairperson beforehand and with other professionals in the conference itself later.

Parents' rights or children's rights

Another dilemma which seems relevant to touch upon in this chapter is the question of the rights of the parents and the rights of the child and of balancing the two. Which should be given greater weight? Is it possible for children's rights to be separated from parental rights? Would children's rights be an issue at all if parents fulfilled their parental duties to their children within an ethical framework of love and care? Archard (1993) argues that children's rights are not 'all-or-nothing' (p. 88) and because children might not have some adult rights does not mean that they have nothing. He develops the idea of the importance in family relationships of both children's rights based on the rights and duties of the parental relationship and the mutual affection which brings 'a warmer sense of "belongingness"' to the child. (p. 89)

Philosophers previously related rights to concepts of duty and obligation but in the 1980s have related it to precisely *what* those duties and obligations are. (Waldron 1984) A feature of the debate is an ethical consideration as to *how* those duties and obligations are carried out. The argument is that it would not be enough to speak of 'natural rights' or 'human rights' without defining the values and principles on which for example, a parent might interpret their duties and obligations to the rearing of their children.

Children used, of course, to have the status of property (Page 1984). 'Parental rights were property rights residing in the father. The mother, being herself property, could have no such rights.' (p. 187) The changes which have occurred in the status of women, in attitudes to the ownership of people, to human rights and to the maltreatment of children, have contributed to the principle that the welfare of the child is paramount. This is a principle enunciated in the Children Act 1989. Nevertheless, what a parent may believe is for the welfare of his/her child, may not be perceived as such by the society in which they live. Examples of this type of dispute often appear within the child protection procedures and might include parents who have severely punished their child with a belt on their bottom or with a cane on the soles of their feet, or have allowed a clitoridectomy to be carried out on their daughters or have left their child alone for long periods of time without a responsible carer. Cases like these could appear in a child protection conference and raise the issue of the forfeiture of parental rights. Page, who writes quite separately from child protection matters, suggests that it is only in cases where the severity of the harm or the seriousness of the danger warrants it, that forfeiture should occur 'not the fact that it is *clear* that some harm is done or that some danger exists.' (p. 189). He further argues that whilst parental rights have many similarities to property rights, yet there is a repulsion on the part of most people to assigning children to the status of property. Instead he suggests that parental rights reflect the kind of special interest parents have in their children particularly in their desire to shape the course of their child's life, and in broad outline to determine the kind of person the child will become. Such a 'desire is not a selfish interest of the parent but bound up with the parent's natural affection for the child and concern for its good.' (p. 195)

He takes the view that a system of parental rights exists because parenthood itself may be described as an activity worthy of being protected and that 'the precise form that the system of parental rights takes, and the detailed content of those rights, will depend on the social and political context in which they exist.' (p. 202)

A more recent examination of parental and children's rights (Bigelow et al 1988) echoes Page's focus on the importance of the activity of parenthood but extends the discussion to include the idea of autonomy of both parents and children. The writers claim there is a logical priority of the separable interests of the child over the autonomy of the parents in the fulfilment of their special responsibilities for and the exercise of their special rights over their children. They suggest the family 'is like a state within a state; interference by the public state within family affairs is a grave matter, comparable to interference by one state in the internal affairs of another.' (p. 185) However, they argue for a paternalistic interference providing it is protectionist and not perfectionist. They describe perfectionist paternalism as 'if adults in general are morally obliged to do what is *best* for their child' and protectionist paternalism as 'if adults in general are morally obliged only to ensure that no *harm* befalls the child.' (p. 185) If the child has some property rights in her/himself as a person, the rights to the property of their own bodies take precedence over the rights of parents to the fruits of their parental labour. When children are very young they cannot exercise the rights of an autonomous person. It is only as the moral relationship between the parent and the child changes, as the child grows and develops that there is a transfer of the autonomy of the parent to the autonomy of the child. 'There is no clear line which the child crosses to become an autonomous adult and the emotional attachments and concerns of parents for their children can make it difficult for parents to curb their inclinations towards interference, however motivated.' (p. 190)

The idea of the gradual change of autonomy from parent to emerging adult in the child, supported by a protectionist paternalistic interference when parental autonomy prevents the child from developing into an autonomous adult, fits well with the ideas underpinning child protection procedures. For example, a child of 13 years who has been the victim of incest over a period of 5 years may disclose the facts to a teacher. The parent may argue that the child was not harmed by the experience, that she did not object to the activity but rather enjoyed the special relationship it created. Nevertheless, the child protection investigation instigated by the teacher would, given sufficient evidence almost certainly lead to the prosecution of the father because he would be deemed to be harming the child by exploiting her for his own needs without the child being mature enough to withhold consent. The chairperson of the child protection conference would ask members to consider registration and a protection plan on the grounds that the parent was harming the child and the child would be in need of the state's protection. 'There must be one or more identifiable incidents which can be described as having adversely affected the child. They may be acts of commission or omission. They can be either physical, sexual, emotional or neglectful.' (Working Together 1991) In effect the decision to register in the conference is a value judgement on behalf of the state about whether what has happened to the individual child is abusive and therefore harmful and would warrant intervention.

Archard (1993) analyses parental rights from the point of view of biological parenthood and moral parenthood. He sees the two aspects lying at the heart of the nature of parenting but that the one does not guarantee the other. 'Moral parenthood is the giving to a child of continuous care, concern and affection with the purpose of helping to secure for it the best possible upbringing.' (p. 109) Unfortunately, as Roche (1989) points out, the openness of the concepts such as 'the best possible upbringing of the child' or 'the child's best interest' or 'the welfare of the child' is socially problematical and may be used by some people to impose their views about what is right for the child on the rest of society. The conference is one such arena where this may occur. It follows therefore that at the very least, the child's views should be presented in the conference. Roche refers to the 'child autonomy' argument being used in the Gillick case, in which a 16 year old girl was found to have the right to decide to use contraception, and that the decision reached was 'a landmark for children's rights' (p. 138) but the case of 'J' (a minor) (Medical Treatment) in July 1992 qualified the Gillick precedent. Lord Donaldson in the Court of Appeal said that the whilst good parenting involved giving minors the maximum degree of decision-making as was prudent, prudence did not involve avoiding all risk but it did involve avoiding risks which, if eventuated, may have irreparable consequences or may be disproportionate to the benefits which accrued from taking them. In this case, one of the peculiarities of anorexia nervosa was that it created a wish not to be cured or only to be cured if and when the patient decided to cure herself, which might well be too late. Roche's concluding comment that 'in the debate about children's rights and the rights of parents and families and professional anxiety about children's welfare there exists no ideal, correct practice,' holds true for child protection conferences. It is this kind of complexity which makes for dilemmas and difficulties in the task of chairing.

Summary

This chapter has cast a glance over the kinds of wider ethical issues involved in the holding of child protection conferences. Time has been spent on them on the grounds that the chairs of conferences need to have considered them, to perform their task fully.

3 The task of conferences in child protection in relation to chairing

> ... *the welfare of the child is the overriding factor guiding child protection work ... and the importance of professionals working in partnership with parents ...*
> (Working Together, 1991)

Working Together guidelines

The guidelines which prescribe conferences are to be found in Working Together (1991). At the time of the interviews with the people who chaired the conferences described in this book, Working Together (1988) was in use. It was debatable whether to start this chapter with the earlier guidelines. However although there are differences in the two versions, the tasks prescribed are similar. (The differences are more fully discussed in chapter 15 with regard to the effect of the earlier version on the activity of chairing.)

The first statement in the 1991 version about the nature of the conference is a little different from the 1988 version. The conference is *not* a 'forum for a formal decision that a person has abused a child', but (para. 6.1) it is for 'sharing information and concerns, analysing risk and recommending responsibility for action'. Much time and energy in the past was spent on identifying how the abuse was caused and who caused it. The weight of the past hung heavily in the present and often unduly influenced the future, regardless of the severity or persistence of the abuse or neglect. In a further paragraph, the purpose of an initial child protection conference is expanded. It should only be called after an investigation under Section 47 of the Children Act 1989 has been made and even then it should be timed only when relevant information and reports are available to inform the decisions of the conference, normally within eight working days, except when there are particular reasons for a delay, for example when it is necessary to carry out an assessment to plan for the future needs of the child. Paragraph 6.5 clarifies the task: 'to bring family members and professionals together; to share and evaluate the information gathered during the investigation; to make decisions about the level of risk to the child/ren; to decide on the need for registration; and to make plans for the future'. Once a decision to register has been made, that is the only decision that a conference is required to make. A named key-worker should be appointed and a core group of professionals to carry out the inter-agency work of the protection plan.

These prescribed tasks are examined in more detail in the following sections.

Attendance

There are factors in attendance at conferences which affect chairing. Who attends, whether it is professionals or parents or both, will directly influence the outcome for the individual child. Every professional who has personal contact with and knowledge of the child should be there, as well as their supervisors when appropriate, and those representatives of the agency with powers over resources and expert advice. It has become increasingly evident that it is crucially important for parents to attend, with a supporter if they wish. Jo Tunnard (in Stainton Rogers et al, 1989 p. 179) emphasises the need for improvement in involving parents in decision-making because there is 'still little told to families about what is happening and no written material' and 'any client of any service should be able to question or challenge decisions made and to enlist the assistance of someone else to help them to do that'. Information from parents themselves, shows unequivocally that they wish to be present in conferences to hear what is being said and to say what they wish to say (Shemmings and Thoburn, 1990, Shemmings, 1991, Thoburn 1992, and Thoburn et al, forthcoming). However, if numbers become cumbersome, there is a diffusion of interest as well as communication problems and quality of discussion and decision-making is affected. Hallett and Stevenson (1980) note the impossibility of gathering every professional to a case conference and recommend written submissions, or the absentee's representative presenting their contributions. When this was attempted as a way of representing parents' views, a local study from Cumbria found in 1990 that despite the opportunity for parents to give their views to the social worker beforehand for her/him to present at the conference, only 42 per cent of the parents did so and 58 per cent did not, so although an apparently effective system was devised for parents to use, they did not; whereas in the conferences attended by parents in a number of other areas where local studies were carried out (Bradford, Dudley, Essex, Hackney, Sheffield, St. Gabriel's Family Centre, Brighton and Wiltshire), the majority of parents questioned thought they were able to put their views satisfactorily. They found it more difficult when their participation was partial (chapter 3, Thoburn 1992). As well as the importance of the presence of the right people at the case conference, consideration needs to be given to the value of what happens as a result of the 'mix'. There are two views in the literature pre parental participation, about the value of 'live' discussion in case conferences to produce important information. One is Hallett and Stevenson's view that 'small, apparently trivial pieces of information assume a significance and coherence when put together with others ...' and the other from Brunel University, cited by Hallett and Birchall (1991) which criticises reliance on the emergence of views from multi-disciplinary discussion and advocates proper preparation and collation of individual opinions before the case conference, by the Social Services Department. One of the advantages of the presence of parents at case conferences, however, is that they act as a foil to professional inaccuracy of data and assumptions. Their contribution to the discussion of the protection plan seems to encourage commitment and responsibility to the plan because they are involved in devising it (Bell and Sinclair 1993). One of the features of early case conferences was the mutual trust believed to facilitate better multi-disciplinary working. In conferences where parents and children are present, experience has shown that open-ness and honesty are essential ingredients. Despite the meeting being formal and following an agenda, parents have said that they could tell that when professionals spoke of negative aspects of their parenting openly, then they knew they were being honest and they could trust what was going on in the conference (Shemmings 1991).

In conferences of professionals only, there are difficulties as outlined by the above criticisms, which tend to diminish the quality of the conference and there are recurring objections made to parental participation in conferences. They include the inhibitive effect on professionals and parents alike, issues of confidentiality, problems of evidence, conflict, poor professional skills and the danger of the conference becoming a pseudo court of law. (Phillips and Evans 1986) With the advent of parental participation in conferences the signs are that a fresh sense of open-ness about the conduct of the procedures facilitates co-operation between professionals and parents in the protection plans for the child and does not adversely affect either information-giving or decision-making. (Thoburn and Shemmings 1990, Burns 1991)

Gathering and assessing information

One of the questions raised by child protection procedures is whether the conference is becoming a substitute for individual professional work. Hallett and Birchall (p. 226) cite the Family Rights Group report that there is 'evidence from practitioners of ... procedures invoked too frequently as a play-safe mechanism, with conferences all too often used, particularly in sexual abuse, to spread anxiety around rather than to plan interventions.' The report also suggested that case discussions outside child protection procedures, which should be 'a normal part of a good case-work service' were being overlooked. In a policy paper of the Society of Clinical Psychiatrists (1985), also quoted by Hallett and Birchall, there is reference to conferences as being 'pernicious and should be abolished: they dangerously diffuse responsibility amongst an unaccountable group. Decisions depending on the professional skills of those directly handling the case are not for discussion in such a group' (p. 226). Dale et al (1986) warn that there is 'no equation for balancing the pros and cons of each available option for an abused child in care: there are no check-lists or computer programmes to replace the 'god-like task of responsible professional judgement' (p. 156).

Similarly, preparing well-considered reports for a conference is essential. A chairperson's standards regarding the quality of the reports should prevail. The investigation needs to be evaluated in readiness for the assessment of risk in the conference. Professional judgement should be made on the assessment prior to the conference. The Rochdale Report (1990) shows that in the 30 sample cases reviewed, the case conferences considered the risk to the child in 77 per cent but that the issue was not addressed in 23 per cent and that there was a tension surrounding case conferences concerning the quality and extent of the work prior to the conferencing. The report suggests that a case conference was often a substitute for an adequately conducted and co-ordinated investigation: that half of the cases were known already to social workers but only six had assessments on file: three files were well written with good assessments and agreements but that often the information in the file was not collated at all. In a number of cases 'the balance of the discussion was to establish that the child had been harmed and that a person was responsible rather than attempting an informed assessment of present and continuing risk.'

As Hallett and Birchall point out, 'the nature of the knowledge of child abuse is problematic on which practitioners base their judgements and actions. There is no more psychopathological evidence for batterers than in the general population' (p. 159). Reports presented to the conference by the social worker should therefore contain a record of the contact with the family, a discussion of the content of the investigation and work, and a professional evaluation of that contact, not, as has happened in the past, unsubstantiated opinion about the incident and the alleged abuser. Ideally it should have been shared beforehand with parents and children, if appropriate. If such vitally important judgements about a child are not made by the professional worker responsible but are being shifted into the general arena of the child protection conference for a free-for-all discussion by everyone, then good social work practice is jeopardised and clients are unlikely to receive the kind of service they need.

Levels of risk

There appears to be a conflict about whether assessing risk in some way deals a disservice to families. On the one hand there is a school of thought that suggests checklists, which indicate particular factors which predispose families to be abusive, should be used, (Greenland 1987) and that identification of risk warrants intervention and that tight management reduces abuse (Creighton 1984a) but on the other hand, there is a vehement school of thought that this brings within the purview of the agencies many families who are not abusive and therefore it is unjust and should be eschewed (Parton 1985, Stevenson, chap. 1, 1989). The view of these writers is that in any descriptions of personal or intrafamilial pathologies, we see profiles of the general population including ourselves. Birchall (Stevenson, chap. 1 1989) says that trying to identify high-risk families is fruitless and even damaging. She goes on to say that despite conference and court defining limits about what is acceptable in terms of parenting and what is not, in practice many decisions about risk are taken by professionals at 'street-level' and there is a wide discrepancy of responses (p. 11). Cooper and Ball (1987) also thought that a too wide and speculative use of At Risk Registers led to more families being brought to the notice of the police through case conferences.

A more practical approach to dealing with levels of risk, is to be found in four books (Moore, 1985; Corby, 1987; Stainton Rogers et al, 1989; and Bannister et al, 1992) which outline risk factors which need to be assessed. Moore says that despite considerable work on the concept of risk, as far as human behaviour is concerned, it is not possible to have a mathematical formula and that even car insurance companies can have categories of high-risk customers but cannot predict who will have an accident. She includes a simple but comprehensive assessment list with physical and emotional risks to be assessed, child, mother, father and vulnerability. Bannister (in Stainton, Rogers et al) also warns about the dangers of looking for risk factors, in that they tend to become self-fulfilling prophecies, but assessing likely risk factors could be helpful in areas such as parental personality, marital and family relationships, vulnerability of the child, social deprivation and the precipitating incident. Print and Dey (in Bannister) describe empowering mothers of sexually abused children, and state that they believe there are several components to risk assessment (p. 64). Details of the child's disclosure, the whereabouts and attitude of the abuser and the attitudes of other family members, as well as the non-abusing parent, are important aspects of the assessment.

Probably most helpful are Corby's suggestions because they are the most focused, although he does not include the child's views. He found that in his observations of case conferences there was no systematic consideration of risk and he recommended assessment in the following areas: parental character, co-operation of the parents, previous history of child abuse, availability of police and medical evidence, seriousness of injury, age/vulnerability of the child and degree of suspicion surrounding the cause of the injury/neglect.

A more recent report on issues for managers in child protection (Evans 1990) paints a pessimistic picture of managers equating the management of risk with caution and safety by adhering to the procedures so closely that professional judgement was restricted. He describes the introduction of what has become known as the 'Orange Book' (Department of Health 1988) leading to angry feelings on the part of managers because of its restrictive views and lack of recognition of workload implications in carrying out such assessments. He found 'an air of unease about risk management surrounding the decision-making process' because of the difficulties of balancing procedural correctness with the exercise of professional judgement. Often when procedures were carried out to the letter, participants found the process unhelpful (pp. 6-7).

Assessment of risk, whilst sounding rather straightforward as part of the task of the chairperson of a conference, raises complex problems for chairing because of the mixed messages it contains about prediction and certainty. A better description of the activity might be 'weighing the balance' between negative and positive information about the family, yet this too must not become a simplistic rehearsal of the professionals' views. Both positive and negative information needs evaluating first and a distinction made between fact and opinion. As Shemmings (in Thoburn 1992) says, most conferences are full of opinion. Providing it is examined carefully, then it can take its proper place in the discussion. He uses some amusing diagrams reminiscent of the TV advertisement test for tender peas, to illustrate how professionals may test their own information.

Decision to register

It is clear in the Guidelines that conferences should make only one decision, and that is whether to register the name of the child or not, in a category of abuse. The problems of decision-making in general will be discussed in the next chapter but there appears to be difficulty for chairs in reaching the decision about registration. (See also chapter 10)

There are problems in consistency of registration, particularly nationally. One child living in one area suffering similar abuse to another child living in another area, may receive very different treatment. Hallett and Birchall quote, for example, rates of new registrations ranging in some areas from 0 to 5.3 per thousand children and in other areas, rates from 10 to 17.5 per thousand from standing cases as well as idiosyncratic demographic differences such as higher rates of registration in Shropshire than Hackney and 10 times as many registrations in Southwark as in Gloucestershire! (p. 223) Any tightening of the guidelines to ensure parity of response in child protection procedures would carry with it the danger of greater bureaucratization and a stifling of creativity or of the innovative use of resources as described above by Evans in his work with managers in child protection.

Corby (1987) found inconsistency too in registration decisions in his analysis of 55 observed case conferences. Decisions made with regard to care proceedings were generally clear but decisions made with regard to registration were not linked to any specific criteria and often the reason would be because of the different professionals' views as to the purpose of the register. These varied as to whether it was a record of concern, a ranking exercise of seriousness of cases, a rationing of scarce resources to priority families, or to ensure for the chairperson that a less than competent social worker would be required to account for her/his work at the review in six months' time. He thought that such a variety of reasons for registering must place doubt on the credibility to be attached to registers (p. 77).

Higginson (Community Care 1990) examined 40 case conferences in an urban local authority and found what she called 'distorted evidence.' Whilst she was not looking solely at the decision to register, nevertheless her findings are significant for chairs because the final decision about registration is based on both the evidence given in the conference and all the previous decisions made regarding that particular family. Moore's comment (1985) that 'Registers have been made into talismen by professionals but in reality are only tools to sharpen up practice' still contains a blast of commonsense and truthfulness about the importance of competent chairing in regard to this one decision of the conference.

The protection plan

A protection plan, if it is to make any sense after the conference and to be of any use to the child requires detailed consideration and decisions based on the assessment of risk of harm to the child, following the sharing of information. To do this adequately necessitates time being spent generating the details of ideas, liaising, co-ordinating, and cross-checking which may be an inappropriate use of the corporate time of the conference. Thus protection plans have tended to be general and limited, covered in the minutes of conferences by words such as 'monitor', 'liaise', 'communicate' and 'co-ordinate', naming a key-worker, and offering a review date. But there are examples of chairs who manage to shape a comprehensive protection plan at the conference and delegate to the agencies resposible for carrying it out (Thoburn et al, forthcoming).

Some local authorities follow the suggestion in Working Together (1991) to nominate a 'core group' to work out the protection plan and where these include parents, a more satisfactory plan is likely to be devised because there is time to do it. It is also less threatening for parents than a full conference and it is possible to produce recorded agreements in them.

Castle (1977) cited in Hallett and Birchall (p. 236) found in a retrospective study of social workers' perceptions of case conferences that there were an unquantified number of occasions when recommendations were not carried out or a majority decision could not be reached. Hallett and Stevenson (1980) found conference members uncertain about the status of the case conference conclusions and Hilgendorf (1981) also cited in Hallett and Birchall (p. 237) observed that case conference conclusions were frequently decisions and that the larger the group the more inclined it was to regard itself as a decision-making body. The Brunel University study (1988 cited in Hallett and Birchall p. 238) noted that the case conference conclusions were often given the status of decisions.

The strength of the recommendations regarding a protection plan may lie in the use of Review conferences because these will ensure whether a plan has been carried out or not. It would take some nerve for a worker to arrive at a conference knowing the recommendations from the initial conference had not been carried out.

Family turbulence

This phrase 'family turbulence' coined by Packman (Packman, et al 1986) describes vividly the volatility and unpredictability of some of the families who become involved in child protection procedures. It is an ingredient not referred to in the guidelines Working Together, but it is a factor in what may happen in a conference whether parents are present or not, which the chairperson should heed. The plans made with 'turbulent families' and for them, often do not transpire because their circumstances change so quickly. Therefore carrying out a protection plan may elude even the most assiduous social worker. It is also possible for the conference itself to be plunged into circular and conflictual discussions about the chaos surrounding such a family. The conference may spend its time simply trying to catch up with what is happening, as the family composition changes or the family moves about geographically, or as decisions which were made originally are overturned. Turbulence may also occur solely as a result of the impact of the procedures, as families try and grapple with the consequences of the allegation of abuse, particularly sexual abuse, and with their fears that their children will be removed (Bannister et al, 1992). Involving parents who are in the grip of a stream of events over which they have little control, should help to provide them with a clearer direction about what is happening and enable the professionals to engage more positively with them. Strong chairing in these circumstances would provide the lead to this.

Summary

There are clear guidelines about the task of chairing, but not about how to do it. The following three chapters address this problem.

4 Chairing and small group dynamics

> *The behavioural patterns [of groups] ... are identical but at different levels of intensity and are certainly susceptible to different degrees of conscious control.* (Tom Douglas, 1983)

Most of the literature on groups and group theory is about therapeutic groups. Nevertheless, some of the ideas are transferable and useful when considering the management of child protection conferences. The child protection conference in Working Together may be described as a business meeting, a work group, a committee or a task group but it is possible that it will manifest some aspects of an ongoing therapeutic group. A chairperson may need to bear in mind that both these group behaviours are likely to be present in a child protection conference.

Task and care of the group

Bales' work on groups in the 1950s, focuses on what he thought were the two main aspects of group behaviour: task and maintenance. He believed that unless these were attended to by the leader of the group then the group would find difficulty in functioning. He also developed useful ideas about roles in groups, pointing out that every member of a regular group tended to take on a particular role in the group to help it function.

A child protection conference is highly likely to have regular members at its meetings and they tend to form an ongoing group within a group. They get to know each other well, discuss cases they have in common, make arrangements for other meetings and may even see each other socially, so they are likely to behave in many ways like an established group with some of its characteristics. The chairperson may need to have as part of her/his resources for chairing skilfully, knowledge about keeping the meeting to its task whilst at the same time being aware when members require therapeutic attention.

A seminal text on small groups and how they function was written by Bion in 1961. His fieldwork was carried out in therapeutic groups. It was the source of his 'basic assumptions' theory in groups, of 'self-preservation' and 'good group spirit.' He described three types of group behaviour resulting from those basic assumptions: fight or flight, pairing and dependence on the group. When contrasting therapeutic groups with work groups, he suggested that the work group behaviour would depend on the 'proto-mental system' which allowed for voluntary co-operation in a work group. The ongoing mental activity is designed to further the task in hand and for a work group to function, it must include this development of thought, intended for translation into action. The aims of a work group, he says, can be 'hindered and occasionally furthered by emotional drives of obscure origin' (p. 188), but he believed such activities could be given cohesion by the group acknowledging the basic assumptions once more, of self-preservation and good group spirit. Many chairs of conferences would be aware of these processes occurring in their meetings and some knowledge of the significance of an unexpected aggressive response (fight) to an issue, or a distancing response (flight), would be advantageous to the chairing task.

Unseen processes in groups

The idea of a group process being beyond the control of the individuals in a group, is developed by Thompson and Kahn (1970) when they observe, 'each member of the group though he may continue to behave in ways which are characteristic of him, is influenced by the behaviour of each of the others and also by the prevailing mood or climate which is present in the group at any moment of time. This mood or climate is something to which he contributes but which he cannot control.' (p. 12) Detecting group processes like those in a committee or conference is difficult, but the authors draw a parallel with similar destructive forces which occur in therapy groups. In committees, they say, they are labelled as 'sticking to one's principles' or 'upholding the rights of minorities' (p. 21). They extract two different, yet rather similar basic assumptions: the wish to be separate and the wish to be one of the group. Together these contain 'a feeling about the powerful and mysterious nature of group forces and an acknowledgement that groups contain potentialities for both benefit and harm to their individual members' (p. 21).

Transposing these ideas to a conference, a chairperson would need to take note of conflicting views likely to divide the conference and draw attention to them and if necessary decide that the issues at variance should be dealt with outside the conference. S/he would also need to take note of what happens to parents in conferences in case they either agree with everything that is being said so as not to be separate from the group or, more likely, to be unaware of the main group thinking so as to be isolated in the conference and perhaps react in a hostile manner, as a result.

Moore (1985) makes the same point when she says 'the group of professional "friends" who attend case conferences regularly develop cohesion and norms which may be difficult to challenge from within' (p. 83).

Tuckman's well-known 'forming, norming, storming, performing' (to which Allan Brown added 'mourning') as a description of the group process (Allan Brown 1979) does not seem to fit readily with case conferences because their membership is variable but should a conference begin to 'form, storm and norm' then a chairperson would need to intervene and return the conference to the task in hand.

Managing a group

Tom Douglas (1983) thought all groups similar with no absolute differences but he adjudged two factors as distinct entities: 'time' and 'leadership behaviour'. At one level, he thought 'groupness' to be about the amount of time people spend together. At another level, decisions made in groups could leave group members in ignorance as to how the decision was reached because whilst they are actively involved in the group they cannot be aware of what is happening to the group as a whole. Understanding, therefore, about what is happening is the responsibility of the chairperson. Data collection from which logically consistent explanations can be made, is a key aspect of this responsibility and he says, the language used by members and the choices made by them need to be clear and simple. Thus the timing of the process is a key factor to enable clarification to take place. Both these aspects of the way a group behaves need to be managed by strong chairing.

He goes on to expand the ideas on unseen group influences as follows: conformity, compliance, identification, internalisation, co-operation and competition. A chairperson who was unaware of the possibility of all these influences being active within a conference would find her/himself at a severe disadvantage in chairing. A chairperson's role is to monitor these influences because they affect outcome. 'Whether or not people take notice of group processes and the other affecting factors in group situations these factors do influence the outcome of group situations and often produce results that in either direction, intensity or nature, have not been allowed for in the calculations of the planners.' (p. 112)

A chairperson needs to have thought out beforehand how to handle situations which might arise from these influences so that s/he is prepared to a certain extent, for disagreement, anxiety, prejudices, lack of proper preparation on the part of members of the conference and confusion on the part of parents attending.

Standards

Douglas makes another point which is highly relevant to conferences when he describes norms in a group as 'the unwritten rules by which the group operates and which serve to maintain its unique identity. In work situations norms create standards.' (p. 116) The chairing of a conference inevitably involves being accountable for standards. Was it a good case conference or was it not? Were the decisions reached the best possible in the circumstances? He sounds a warning note: 'Decisions will be affected by group influences that are not apparent: they will be made with all sincerity as objectively based on available data, and yet they will be the result of the interaction of a complex mesh of motives and perceptions, of considerations, of possible consequences and of awareness of some pressures and of ignorance of others' (p. 232).

Moore (1985, p. 85) refers similarly, to the psycho-analytical concept of a group like a case conference mirroring the family it is concerned about, by playing out the issues of role, conflicts, child as victim or provoker, rights of parents or rights of child, legalistic or therapeutic interventions, as well as political philosophies and societal aims, much as Douglas described the unseen influences at work in a group. She cautions against chairs being line managers because of the difficulties of keeping objective standards in the conference.

Dale et al (1986) echo these ideas with their concept of dangerousness which they see applying within agencies and in case conferences, in the same way as it applies to families, and Mitchell (1989) also specifically links small group theory with case conferences by suggesting that members of case conferences are controlled by the standards set by the group which would be different from those set by participants when outside the group. He suggests that one of the dangerous ways for a case conference to act, is by bracketing off realities experienced by the family such as poverty, environmental problems, race, and class and only looking at the evil of abuse. He speaks of 'emotional contagion' in a group and of the way in which case conferences are highly susceptible to seizure, disintegration and disruption by individual members controlling the quality, amount and spread of information. By making caucuses and alliances members can highjack standards and decisions which the chairperson needs to keep within her/his authority.

Seeking consensus and the consequences of groupthink

Moore (1985) describing case conferences (p. 83) introduces the idea that pursuing consensus in a group is not fruitful because unanimity does not equal truth. She also refers to the group influences which make members eager to conform to achieve consensus. Phillips et al (1979) set out previously the dangers of adopting consensus as an ideal in their more general book on leadership and this will be returned to later in the chapter on leadership skills.

A final aspect of group behaviour, which chairs need to take account of when chairing conferences, is 'groupthink'. This is a concept described by Janis and Mann (1977) as 'a drive for consensus at the cost of realistic consideration of alternative ideas.' A chairperson would need to spot the following symptoms: concurrence seeking norms, an illusion of invulnerability – that the group is beyond reproach, rationalisation – minimising evidence that threatens the group's basic assumptions, and developing and prompting negative stereotypes of outsiders. They give some correctives to 'groupthink', which would provide useful strategies for chairs of conferences. They are: coping with different levels of status in the group by asking questions, challenging the prevailing wisdom of the group to produce different information, developing a norm where disagreement or clash of opinion is acceptable in the discussion.

Summary

There appears to be sufficient evidence in the literature on small groups to suggest that a chairperson of a child protection conference needs to take note of some of the theories available, to enable her/him to approach the task of chairing with clear ideas about what is likely to occur and some strategies for dealing with it, particularly with regard to the task of the group, the unseen processes and how to manage them, standards and the influences of consensus and groupthink.

5 Decision-making and chairing

> *Policy and practice in child abuse both influence and depend upon the wider context of services for children and their families and sophisticated decision-making can never be a substitute for welfare provision.* (Jean Packman, 1989)

Working Together (1988 and 1991) says that the only decision to be made by the initial child protection conference is whether to register the child or not. It makes it sound as though making the decision is akin to plucking it out of the air. The literature on decision-making shows that all decisions are made up of what has gone before, including previous decisions, so a chairperson with responsibility to make an important decision such as the one about registration, needs to have some knowledge of the mechanics of how to reach a decision in a group setting.

There are some well-worn phrases used in connection with decision-making and they are worth examining first.

'Risky shift' and 'the more information the better'

In 1964, a study carried out by the University of Michigan, called into question the idea that group decision-making provided a 'checks and balances' function, and created a conservative consensus. The experiment suggested that as a result of the diffusion of responsibility in the group, which in its turn derived from the factor of maximum communication, there was a group-induced shift toward greater risk-taking, produced by the pressures toward consensus in decision-making. This interesting phenomenon, known as the 'risky shift' was demonstrated by male college students making decisions that involved actual risks and payoffs leading to greater risk-taking which occurred in the absence of discussion and consensus. The mechanism underlying the group-induced shift towards greater risk-taking, consisted of a spread of responsibility particularly among status equals. Were this to be found to be true in relation to decisions made in child protection conferences, the consequences would be alarming. However, the experiment was repeated by Gibb in 1989 (Hallett and Birchall 1991) and she modified the finding to a shift to one extremity or the other, either to risk or caution. Even so, a decision at one extreme or another is not helpful.

A chairperson would need to ensure that all the professionals took open responsibility for their views as to whether to register or not. It is one of the tasks which is notoriously difficult to chair because members of the conference tend to distance themselves from the decision, at the point of making it.

Another study of decision-making by probation officers in relation to information about their cases, made in 1964, called into question the prevalent idea that the more information that was made available, the better the decision. It showed, on the contrary, that providing brief but accurate summaries of information led to confident and competent decision-making. The experiment took actual summaries from the probation officers' case records and divided them onto cards with descriptions of the full information written on the edge of the cards. The probation officers were asked to select from the summaries and from the full information, to make the best decisions and the two were compared. The way the cards were selected showed that the greater the information the more the problem was obscured and instead of decisions improving, the increased complexity led to less effective decisions.

One of the main tasks of a conference is the information gathering. The role of the chairperson is to clarify the information so that the incident of abuse or neglect is not obscured but emerges clearly. Sometimes professionals arrive at a conference ready to divulge every piece of information they have gleaned in connection with the family. If the conference is deluged with it, clarifying what is relevant to the abuse/neglect is a major task for the chairperson. Another aspect of the chairperson's role is in setting standards in the conferences. They may insist that the reports for the conferences are relevant to the occasion and substantiated and evaluated. The formula used by many chairs of summarising the information as the conference proceeds, is also a useful way of controlling the amount of information and editing out irrelevancies.

Ways to manage decision-making

Janis and Mann (1977) describe a theory of how people cope with decisional conflicts, from their extensive research on the psychology of stress. They define a decision as having real life consequences i.e. when the decision-maker is committed to a line of action; and they believe that the principles of decision-making with such consequences are different from those governing verbalised choices on non-consequential issues. They think that the quality of decision-making depends on the quality of decision-making procedures and they list 7 major criteria:

1) a wide range of alternative courses of action should be canvassed;
2) the full range of objectives to be fulfilled and the values implicated should be surveyed;
3) the positive and negative consequences that could flow from the decision should be weighed;
4) new information should be searched for;
5) the new information should be correctly assimilated and taken account of;
6) the positive and negative consequences should be weighed again;
7) detailed provision for implementing the chosen course should be made with contingency plans.

This list mirrors accurately the descriptions given to me by a number of chairs in this study of their own methods of chairing, which they have arrived at mostly from their own experience of chairing rather than training. (See chapter 10)

In contrast to the Michigan study, Janis and Mann advocate that group decision-making is likely to be more positive and will have greater commitment to it when it is made in public. They recommend four types of intervention to improve decision-making: firstly, decision counselling i.e. diagnostic interviews about the information; secondly, assessing the expectation about changing/not changing; thirdly, recognising that conflicts and disagreements can be productive and fourthly using procedures to counteract 'group-think'.

A big decision is made up of little decisions

Parry and Morris (1982, p. 25) use the analogy of Chinese boxes for decision-making. 'We have suggested that a decision is a performative utterance discernible according to certain rules. This is *the* decision. But clearly this may be a mere "imprimatur." The decision is the large "box" which contains the lesser decision boxes ... there is a distinction between the formal structure of power relationships. Clearly the more the "decisional" approach confines itself to formal decisions the more it overlooks the informal.'

Their idea encapsulates the variety of pre-conference decisions which are made before initial child protection conferences. Practice varies from local authority to local authority. Some hold discussions between the social worker and the team manager; some between the social worker and the chairperson; and some between the chairperson and the team manager. Some hold a planning meeting or strategy meeting of staff from some of the agencies and these may be chaired by the social worker or the team manager. It is possible to question at this point, how genuine is the participation by parents at the initial case conference if decisions like these have been made beforehand? However, there is some evidence from research into parents' views, (Shemmings 1991) to suggest that parents can accept that professionals have their own work to do during an investigation of abuse and providing they are informed about the outcome, even if they disagree with it, they are satisfied.

A study of decision-making from the business world (Organisation Studies Journal 1990 pp. 1-16) underlines the findings of many of the early studies with 'an organisational decision is in reality a constellation or a galaxy of numerous individual decisions,' and 'the fundamental problem with decisions is the difficulty of identifying commitment in the collective context of an organisation.' Their discussion highlights the relevance of the human psyche, a factor not mentioned in the early studies. 'When and where a decision begins and ends is not always clear. Some of the decisions are registered in the book of the organisational activities, while others remain hidden in the inner sanctum of the human psyche.' An executive of General Motors is quoted as saying, 'We use an iterative process to make a series of tentative decisions on the way we think the market will go. As we get more data we modify these continuously. It is often difficult to say who decided something and when ... or even who originated a decision. I frequently don't know when a decision is made in General Motors. I don't remember being in a committee meeting when things came to a vote. Usually someone will simply summarise a developing position. Everyone else either nods or states his particular terms of consensus ... Here, then, commitment (i.e. to the decision) has to be traced back to someone's mind, indeed perhaps even to that person's subconscious, and that can become rather problematic.' The parallels between that process used in General Motors and the process of a child protection conference is interesting and illustrates the kind of intuitive awareness that a chairperson needs to tune in to, in order to gather all the information into the conference.

A study of competence and velocity in decision-making in 'high-tech' businesses (Academy of Management Journal 1989, pp. 516-542) offers useful parallels for child protection conferences. Although speed of decision-making is not what child protection conferences are about, nevertheless a glance at their findings shows similarities with other earlier decision-making studies.

The study found that a high level of comprehensiveness slows the strategic decision process, so that the consideration of fewer alternatives and obtaining input from fewer sources leading to a more limited analysis creates quicker decisions. Involvement by many decision-makers lengthens the decision process; limited conflicts speed decisions; conflict triggers interruptions in the decision process and slows the pace. These findings are not startling but given the need for speed in modern business decisions the subsequent propositions are worth taking note of in relation to child protection conference decisions because of the frequent criticisms about the amount of time professional workers involved in child protection procedures, spend in meetings.

The researcher, Eisenhardt, asks, 'How do decision-makers maintain decision quality while moving quickly?' She makes five propositions which link five different factors to the greater speed of the decision process:

1) The greater the use of 'real time' information ('real time' information is where there is little or no time lag between occurrence and reporting).

2) The greater the number of alternatives considered simultaneously (competence in the decision includes exhaustive generation and evaluation of alternatives).

3) The greater the use of experienced counsellors (gathering advice is a key factor: advice is two-tier, from all top management teams plus one or two very experienced executives (counsellors)).

4) The greater the use of active conflict resolution (there was no pattern linking decision speed to either general level of conflict within a team or conflict on the decision BUT conflict resolution was crucial).

5) The greater the integration among the decisions (there is a critical difference between fast and slow decisions lying in the web of relations among decisions. Fast teams related the final decisions to other decisions and plans. Slow teams treated the decisions as discrete and even disconnected.).

Chairs could actively use the advice in 1) to track the route of an incident of abuse; in 3) to invite specialists to help the conference and in 5) to summarise as the conference goes along.

Eisenhardt goes on to say that learning to take fast decisions is important and that 'an emergent perspective highlights emotion as integral to high-stakes decision-making'. She identifies confidence and anxiety as key factors influencing the pace of decision closure and that emotion is therefore critical for understanding decision-making. Handling the emotional content of a conference is not new to chairs in child protection but perhaps it is reassuring that even in high-tech businesses the difficulties of chairing the decision-making are the same.

Social services decision-making

Turning now to the studies of decision-making in child care and child protection, we find most of them highly critical and rather depressing reading (Williams, 1968; Dale et al, 1986; Corby and Mills, 1986; Corby, 1987; Morgan, 1989; Hallett and Birchall, 1991; and Dingwall, Eeekalaar and Murray, 1983; Sinclair, 1984; Bryer, 1988).

The study by Williams on child care decision-making makes a number of criticisms of how decisions are made (p. 50). 'The reasons for decisions were not made explicit; decisions were made on an ad hoc basis; there was a shortage of factual information on which decisions were based; decisions were too influenced by the emotions of those making them; a lack of standardisation, poor communication and lack of feedback as to reasons for successful/unsuccessful decisions.'

The parallel here for conference responses is obvious regarding the need for the chairperson to have clarity about the information presented by different professional workers before fair and appropriate decisions can be made for the child. In the report on Maria Mehmedagi there are detailed criticisms of the decision-making process, concluding with 'Case conferences were dictated by pressure of work rather than policy.'

Dingwall, Eekalaar and Murray used the now well-known phrase the 'rule of optimism' to describe decision-making in case conferences by professional workers. Their analysis of decision-making in child protection procedures showed a rarity in allegations of mistreatment because of a belief in cultural relativism and natural love, which they thought should be overturned. Professionals tend to reflect in conferences, society's views in general so a chairperson would need to keep a tight rein on optimism which was not related to information about the family, the legal system and the local community culture of parenting.

The NSPCC's Rochdale team set out clearly the heavy responsibility of the social worker in making child protection decisions. Their style contrasts with the other rather clinical work on decisions in child care. 'Decisions have tremendous implications for the child's future life, identity and personality and are perhaps the most awesome within the sphere of the social work profession.' (p. 120) 'It is crucial that such decisions be taken carefully in the light of the best information and advice available; that they be primarily child-focused; that they be taken in good faith and that they be open to examination in the courts.' (p. 121) They give priority to needing a clear understanding of the abuse and how it happened and of the levels of physical safety of the child and they conclude, 'There are rarely any simple and obvious solutions – decisions may often involve "a balance of negatives" where the principle is to choose the least detrimental alternative for the long-term prospect of the child.' (p. 156)

Corby and Mills, in an article on 55 case conferences held in one borough between 1981 and 1984 focused on rationality in the decision-making process and found as did Williams 20 years before that there were few explicit criteria for making decisions and that the need to register, confused the issues. They concluded by recommending instead, a focus on risk factors and then appropriate resources to be made available. They noted that conflicts between agencies seriously interfered with decision-making and that stereotyping of other professionals undermined co-operation and led to distortion of professional judgements. They were largely critical of the system they observed as a mechanism for dealing with family problems but despite this say '69 per cent of the cases had not been the subject of further case conferences 2 years later and a further 7 per cent had been the subject of only one further case conference, suggesting that in 3/4 of the cases the system had made good decisions.' They attributed this to a 'concerted and cautious response' by the professionals and that greater clarity about cataloguing concerns 'would improve decision-making and case management not only in the areas discussed but also in hazardous decisions.'

In his later book Corby says 'as a rational decision-making body the case conference left much to be desired' and he urges that there is 'a pressing need for case conferences to develop a more systematic and explicit approach to decision-making' (p. 133).

Sinclair, in her literature search in connection with child care review systems selects Hardiker and Barker's model (1981) of decision-making in five stages for use in Social Services: understanding the problem; identification of objectives; identification of alternative solutions; evaluation of alternatives and choice. She finds it a logical model and similar to the classic decision-making trees. She adds two other types of decision-making: 'routine and fundamental' as the most important aspects which count and she argues for a team or case conference approach to reviewing. She says (p. 23), 'In the long run this may be more economical since it can prevent confusion, provide a better basis for planning and facilitate good working relationships and communications.'

Bryer repeats the Chinese box idea that 'One decision is made up of many others before and brings many others after' (p. 35) and selects two types of decisions rather like Sinclair, 'turning point decisions and maintenance decisions,' as well as describing the content of decisions as 'risk-taking, compromise and consensus' (p. 370).

Morgan shows how the practical aspects of child protection work guidelines in many social work texts, are subject to private and subtle influences. One of her illustrations for this is listing descriptions of case conferences made by researchers. 'Not a place where decisions are made but where they are ratified,' Vernon and Fruin; 'A ritual for self-protection,' Jones et al; 'A formal occasion to leave a permanent record,' Dingwall; 'To test evidence,' Hoggett and Pearl; 'Group processes may be more powerful than the issues discussed,' Dale et al. The list reveals the wide interpretations put upon conferences to describe more subtle and hidden agendas referred to already.

In their comprehensive chapter on 'Decision Processes' Hallett and Birchall also pick out how difficult the search for substantive judgement is, even in the hands of skilled professionals. 'Judgement is a complex process of gathering information and interpreting it, frequently in situations of great pressure, seeking a proper awareness and a disciplined use of one's personal values and experiences' (p. 234). They also trawl the literature on better risk assessment to improve decision-making, citing the poor evidence presented in courts for 'proper development' cases, the dangers of conformity in group decision-making, and the limits to human competence in evaluating complex information and deciding on appropriate responses.

Summary

There are distinctions to be drawn between making decisions on an ad hoc basis, speedy decision-making and effective decision-making. For effective decision-making, a chairperson should have access to the work on classic decision-making, in particular the usefulness of tracking and summarising previous decisions so that the information as it develops, is open and 'on the table' for all members of the conference. Evaluating the information in terms of the risk of continuing harm to the child is essential; and canvassing all the options and their consequences allows for full consideration of advantages and disadvantages as well as being fair to parents.

6 The techniques and skills of chairing

Of a good leader
When his task is finished
His goal achieved
They will say
'We did this ourselves'.
(Lao-tse – a Chinese philosopher)

The origins of chairing

Historically it seems likely that our use of the word 'chair' to mean presiding over a meeting has derived from the Speaker's Chair in the House of Commons, though the Oxford Dictionary says that the word 'chair' derives from the French 'chaire' meaning 'pulpit'. But in 1547 the 'Commons House of Parliament' moved from the Chapter House at Westminster Abbey to St. Stephen's Chapel and it was this move which established the position of the Speaker's Chair. The new location in the Palace of Westminster was assigned by Edward VI and the Chair in which the Speaker sat was placed where the altar had been. The mountings may still be seen. The position of the Chair was such that it was elevated above the level of the members' benches giving the Speaker a commanding position in the Chamber. It also had a space behind it which still exists and is of constitutional importance, as the discussions which take place there are regarded as being outside the Chamber and therefore not part of the proceedings of the House (Wade 1978, p. 1-2). If the concept of chairing did derive from this source then it is perhaps permissible to assume three aspects of the role of the Speaker at the time which remain significant for chairing now. He was acknowledged as having a unique and differing role from the members and one with authority. He was positioned to see everything and be seen by everyone. Outside of the domain of action he had a role in clarifying and gathering information for the Chamber. These aspects of the role of the chairperson will be explored in more general terms from other sources, notably the literature on meetings but also the social work literature.

Role of the chairperson

There is a longstanding popular literature available to aspiring chairs which contains useful advice for chairing any meeting. One of these, a small handbook for chairmen, written anonymously in 1958 firmly says, 'The success of a meeting depends, in a considerable measure, on the capabilities of the chairman. We might almost claim that it succeeds or fails according to his abilities ... The chief duty of a chairman is to conduct the meeting to see that all sides have a fair hearing, and to close the debates when no useful purpose will be served in letting them run on.' (p. 15)

An American book, written in a similar popular style but based on research into conducting meetings, also recognises the key role of the chairperson in running the meeting (Strauss and Strauss 1964). The authors outline the view that although the chairperson is distinctly the leader, their job is not to control. Instead it is 'to help all the members to contribute to the solving of the group's problem. And the members' job is to share in this.' (p. 16) Together the meeting should contain 'all of the knowledge, experience and ability needed to enable it to get what or where it wants' (p. 21). The meeting will not need controlling but enabling and the writers list some leadership functions which are relevant to chairing. They suggest six are shared with the meeting and six which are not shared. These twelve ideas for chairs contain practical wisdom which applies equally well to child protection conferences. Although child protection conferences are now formal business meetings, they also need to operate in an ambience of openness so that parents may participate more fully.

The shared functions suggested by Strauss and Strauss are: creating and monitoring a permissive atmosphere to facilitate freedom to talk; setting the group's goals; getting real consideration for all points of view; keeping the discussion focused towards a solution of the problem being explored; summarising the discussion when it is confused, out of hand, stalemated or too much too fast; and then exploring the group's activities to find ways to improve them.

The functions they suggest are not for sharing are: group stimulator and guide; ensure understanding of the area in which the group has the authority to act; control (with group consent) the way the discussion proceeds, maintain it and suggest different techniques; develop good morale and teamwork; facilitate the solution to conflict; and obtain guidance and support from a higher authority.

The authors provide a further set of lists to enrich and organise group thinking, to improve analysis of problems and ways to promote group solidarity and progress. They embrace the classic decision-making ideas of the previous chapter but describe how to do it.

To enrich group thinking the chairperson should suggest new ideas, raise questions that push on the discussion, try to make the meaning of various suggestions clear, and summarise by getting the group back on line and pulling related suggestions together.

To improve analysis of problems the chairperson should ask questions which help bring out pertinent facts, contribute data that improves members' knowledge and understanding, ask questions or make statements to bring out the fine points and the reasons behind the obstacles and think up situations and questions to bring out the knowledge of the other members.

To increase group solidarity and progress the chairperson should encourage members to be honest, keep an open mind, and modify her/his own viewpoint, find ways to reconcile clashing viewpoints, keep contribution on a reasoning basis and push the group to better/faster action.

'Leading meetings successfully, means changing the thinking and habits of the people involved. This is one of the most difficult jobs because people don't want to change. It requires thinking and planning and help.' (pp. 84-85)

These comprehensive tips for chairing also take account of the tasks required of a child protection conference chairperson. They clarify the importance of stepping into a role different from the other members of the conference, of developing skills which objectify the content and process of the meeting, of acting with authority and indicate the necessity for the independence of the chairperson so that s/he may carry out chairing actions at an optimum level. They are also neatly laid out in a small booklet produced by The Industrial Society, 'Effective Meetings'.

Leadership

A question about chairing which springs immediately to mind is whether there are certain attributes a chairperson might have or acquire. Turning to the literature describing qualities which make for leaders, Phillips et al (1979) produce a convenient chronological analysis of leadership theories starting with the 'great man'/'leaders are born not made' theory, to styles of leadership which may be consciously adopted to suit the group whether authoritarian, laissez-faire or democratic, then noting the situations which demand a particular leader, to functions which demand performance by a leader and the contingencies which demand that style and situation join together to produce a leader. Whilst it is tempting to equate leadership solely with personality, a chairperson of a child protection conference could adopt leadership of style, function and situation and adequately fulfil the chairing role. They are skills which may be consciously acquired.

Allan Brown writing about groups (1979) covers the same theories and concludes, 'Studies show that most individuals tend to be either more task-oriented or more relationship-oriented in their natural styles, though some have an even balance between the two' (p. 49). A child protection conference will ideally include both types of leadership to address the different aspects of the conference. Some of the chairs who were interviewed were aware of the need to be task-oriented but several described a relationship-oriented style which they used. They seemed to lean naturally to the style which suited their personality. Having access to information about both styles and being able to develop skills for using both styles appropriately, would be an added asset to chairs.

Phillips et al go on to say they believe 'leadership should be a dynamic and adaptive process,' and that 'people can become effective by learning techniques of leadership' (p. 78). They believe effective leaders 'are those who have a wide repertoire of self-presentations; they know how to act as they need to, when they need to' (p. 79). This idea fits well with social work training and the experience of being able to respond to clients in a variety of ways on different occasions using a repertoire of roles according to the requirements of the problem.

Similar useful acts for leaders are described by Douglas (1983) but he comes out in favour of a directional style of leadership in time-limited groups. They 'need expert co-ordination to avoid wasting time on unproductive manoeuvres. That means a directive, controlling leadership pattern is exploited. They [committees] contain members with diffuse aims, often enough irreconcilable, so an imposed structure is necessary, that creates artificial but agreed boundaries within which even conflicting interest groups can work if not together exactly, at least not in open confrontation. This kind of ritual structure of necessity inhibits the open agendas and probable sabotage' (p. 149). 'Committees can deal with information ... but they cannot deal with emotional problems very well because their own emotional stability is not and cannot be built into their formal procedural structures' (p. 201). He does not accept the idea that it is possible to deal with the matters of the 'human psyche' brought into a time limited meeting by its members. He sees leadership being a 'constraining factor' in those circumstances. None of the other writers pretend that dealing with the emotional issues is an easy task, but nevertheless they hold the view that leadership skills can be tackled whatever problems are presented providing the leaders are prepared. Douglas's ideas seem to be the most useful for child protection conferences because of the shift in style in conference since parents are included. They may no longer be the rambling therapeutic type of case discussions of the past but are more formal business-like meetings. They are likely to contain suppressed emotion because of the nature of abuse and neglect in relation to a child and thus a more assertive style of chairing is required notwithstanding the importance of an intuitive function to monitor emotions which might overwhelm the conference and its decision-making.

Preparation

Phillips et al (1979) devote two chapters to preparation for leading and how leaders lead. They give four major aspects to preparation (p. 82):

1) the issues or agenda must be foreseen (must understand the context of the problem);

2) the group and individual members must be analysed (what is the level of their understanding of the problem);

3) the physical situation in which the group will meet must be anticipated (tables, ashtrays, drinks, toilets, pencils and paper);

4) the leader's personal style must be appropriately selected (they should have an accurate picture of their impact as a leader);

and then five actions as to how leaders lead (p. 88). In informal language:

1) how to win them over;

2) praise and encouragement;

3) good group spirit;

4) ask questions about the information presented, alternative decisions, etc;

5) enumerate items of business, summarise.

This advice also echoes earlier advice and whilst the literature on chairing skills is in general sparse, what is available, although written some time ago, offers down-to-earth and congruent advice about chairing any meeting. If a chairperson of a child protection conference were to use only this information and no other, s/he would be well informed about how to perform the task.

The body of literature available on chairing conferences in a social work context is more rewarding but nevertheless, still limited with regard to observed studies of conferences as opposed to commentaries and advice on them.

Chairing conferences and reviews in child care social work

The emphasis moves in this literature from theories of leadership to the practicalities of chairing and good ideas. Sinclair (1984) lists 12 phrases which were used to describe the nature of chairmanship (p. 91) within the Child Care Review system. They include having prior knowledge of the case, exploring new approaches, asking for the children's wishes and probing the social work input. The notable differences in her list from the general lists of leadership skills, is the emphasis on hearing the views of the child concerned, providing resources and being clear who will be held accountable. All of these are relevant to a child protection chairperson.

Moore (1985) comments on practicalities for chairs within child abuse work. She thinks chairing should be a free-lance part-time post to give objectivity to it, and she poses the question, 'If the chairperson is allied by professional loyalty to any other members of the case conference, which loyalty does s/he put first?' Her 'tasks for the Chair' mainly follow the lines of the group leadership lists but are firmly focused on details related to the abuse or neglect. 'Is the child abused or at risk? Who will tell the family about registration? Who will be the key-worker? What will the care strategy be? Are the details of family structure, spelling of names, dates of birth, medical/psychiatric histories accurate?'. She also notes that emotional factors need dealing with in conferences. 'A skilled chair knows if and when to make interpretations about what is going on in the group: when to interpret a worker's personal feelings to another or an agency's view which might be inhibiting the conference; when to reveal denial taking place or appropriate confrontation being avoided; when the group is in the grip of a dominant idea and when to bring the meeting back to relevant issues; whether to increase or diffuse anxiety.' (p. 89) Easier said than done! Such emotional content is likely to be better dealt with outside the conference. It should not be ignored but acknowledged and a plan made accordingly. For example, in a conference where a head teacher became angry because social services had not responded to his referral of a child according, in his view, to the procedures, the chair should have firmly accepted the criticism but equally firmly referred it out of the conference to be dealt with later.

The Beckford Report (1987) criticises the practice of line managers chairing case conferences and urges the principle of objectivity to be taken seriously by chairs so that by being independent, any conscious or unconscious alliances would be more likely to be avoided and the safety of the child focused on more clearly.

The problem of retaining objectivity as a chairperson was assessed by Kendrick and Mapstone in relation to the chairing of Child Care Reviews in Scotland (1989 pp. 277-289), and located firmly at the intersection of two variables – the position of the chair in terms of the structure of the social work department and the delegation of the role of the chair in terms of whether it was in the department or carried out by a number of different people at different levels of the department. Their findings suggest that objectivity depends on the chairperson being outside the line management and of sufficiently high status to challenge members of the review body.

It is Corby, however (1987), who specifically researched conferences in relation to child abuse and neglect. He thought that the skills needed by the chairperson were linked to the question of authority in the meeting. He thought the authority within the conference, as expressed by the members, was derived from a number of sources: knowledge and expertise; material resources; legitimate authority (the power in a role); status and reputation; charisma and personal attractiveness; control over information flow and established relationships. He observed all of these operating in case conferences and thought they caused conferences to be uneven, competitive and might cause panic. He concluded that the chairperson was responsible for knowing they existed and therefore finding ways to handle them when they arose. He also found evidence to suggest that case conferences were not achieving the tasks they were intended to achieve. He considered the chairs to hold some responsibility for this too. Inter-agency communication tended to revert to stereotyping and because the chairperson did not have authority over the other disciplines, it was likely that the conference decisions were more binding over social workers than others. He described a picture of confusion and disagreement in case conferences rarely evidenced in open conflict, but reaching its peak over the issue of whether equal weight should be given to parental rights or to the protection of the child. The chairperson's own authority tended to reside in their experience of seeing a range of cases and developing a rating scale about child abuse and neglect not available to the other members and not measurable by external standards and often not declared.

These criticisms were made about conferences when parents were not present. Their presence currently means that professionals have had to change their presentations in conferences as a consequence. Members need to be well prepared and should have shared their reports with parents beforehand. There is greater focus on the use of language and a recognition that opinion is not enough. Evidence and comments have to be substantiated. There is closer working together between the agencies, particularly between the police and social services in investigating cases of sexual abuse and therefore there is less likelihood of stereotyping but there remains the issue of parental rights or the protection of the child. This was referred to by a number of the chairs in this study and remains a central issue for chairing.

Higginson (1990) criticises the lack of substantiated evidence in conferences. She found that chairs allowed some evidence to be ignored, for conclusions to be drawn beyond the evidence presented, for potentially negative information to be consistently presented positively and vice versa without being questioned, for unsubstantiated allegations to go unchallenged, for moral judgements to be made, for professionals to contradict their own evidence and to silence one another, and for illogical evidence to be chosen to make a decision about severity or risk. She suggests that in order to check this tendency there needs to be 'a greater use of more evidential methods throughout the assessment process.'

Similar criticism appears in the Social Services Inspectorate Report on Child Protection Services in Manchester (1990). 'In their reading of case files, Inspectors found in case conference minutes, there was often little distinction between fact and opinion, assertions and assumptions' (p. 16). The Inspectors also attended a number of case conferences and saw that styles of chairmanship varied substantially. 'There is a need to clarify the role of the chair emphasising the importance of enabling checking out, summarising and ensuring an agreed decision is reached.' (para. 7.17) They go on to say (para. 7.18), 'Care should be taken to ensure that the recommendations of the case conference are specific and provide a basis for the development of the case plan. Generalisation, jargon and well-worn phrases should be avoided.'

And again in the Rochdale Report (1991, p. 25) criticism is made that the chair failed to remain objective in 20 per cent of the cases and became over-involved and sought to influence decisions according to his/her views. They made introductions in only 23 per cent of cases, identified participating agencies' power and responsibility in only 43 per cent of cases, clarified the law in only 37 per cent of cases and identified who was to notify parents of decisions in only 47 per cent of cases. The Inspectors considered that the issue of risk had not been addressed in 23 per cent of cases and that 'the policy of mandatory registration was therefore in danger of being interpreted in such a way that all children where non-accidental injury had occurred were automatically put on the register, even where there was every indication that the child was no longer at risk' (p. 22). A number of children were registered where no future work was identified. Where there were a number of children in the family the Inspectors found it difficult to follow the history of one particular child and recommended that consideration of each child be followed through to a decision. This information was evaluated from the minutes.

On the positive side, in 63 per cent of cases the chair had ensured the purpose of the conference was clear; in 70 per cent of cases they enabled all to contribute and in 63 per cent of cases they kept discussion relevant. The emphasis in Working Together (1991), when registration is considered, is on the two requirements for registration and then the allocation to a category of abuse. If chairs were only to be assertive at this point they would demonstrate leadership qualities which would focus the conference on its decision-making and would affect outcome for the child and family in a more direct and open manner.

Hallett and Birchall (1991) gather together the critical comments about chairing from a number of sources. 'There have been recurring concerns that conferences chaired by the social worker's immediate senior lack sufficient distance and objectivity' and 'the facile acceptance of unsubstantiated value judgements' lowers the standards of chairing, ' "below the table" activity causes conferences to be contradictory, not disclosing dissent but acting it out in practice unless the chairperson is able to deal with it'. They think that although Working Together (1988) recommends greater skill in chairing, more important is preparation and networking by the chairperson and the key-worker beforehand.

Accumulated criticisms like these are rather depressing to read but it is possible to use them positively, by compiling from them a list of tips for better practice: preparation is necessary; evidence should be substantiated; clarification by checking and summarising is important; agreement by the whole conference on risk, registration and recommendation should be sought; dissent and emotional undertones need to be brought out; and creativity should be a priority. All of the criticisms could be dealt with if chairs were to adopt the skills described in the literature on small groups, decision-making and leadership. Chapters by Baxter and by Monk in Thoburn (1992) about chairing conferences with parents attending, brighten what has become a doleful list of ineptitudes. They write from their own experiences of chairing, giving positive ideas without diminishing the difficulties.

Summary

There are leadership skills which may be defined and learned, whether for general meetings or for child protection conferences. The criticisms of the chairing of conferences in child protection could also be addressed by turning them round to use positively rather than negatively.

Part II

Part II

7 Methodological framework

Individuals are conceptualised as active agents in constructing and making sense of the realities they encounter rather than responding in a robot-like fashion according to role expectations established by social structures.
(W. J. Filstead, 1979)

First ideas

Child abuse and neglect is a complex and difficult subject in itself and it raises connected issues, such as domestic violence, cultural differences in child-rearing, social disadvantage, family relationships, and, in dealing with it, issues of rights of family members. Familiarity with all of these subjects would be useful to chairs when chairing but would they regard such resources as important or even relevant? In writing the thesis from which this book springs these subjects were explored in relation to the chairs' attitudes and whether such issues influenced them in the way they conducted the conferences.

The idea of conferences being the expression of the boundary between the family and the state and where public attitudes to childhood and the treatment of children were defined, was thought provoking. Were they the arena in which standards about parental behaviour were tested? Did they make a contribution to society's standards about what is acceptable or legal in parenting in this country? Would the chairperson of a child protection conference have similar views and see themselves as having a role in establishing standards?

Parental and child participation in conferences was an important aspect to consider because of the current focus in the child protection debate. What did the chairs think of it?

How did the chairs run their conferences? What did they do? From the literature on groups, decision-making and chairing skills, an optimal use of skills was available which if used by chairs, would mean they would chair well. It would be interesting to discover whether the chairpersons had arrived at any of this knowledge and whether, if they had, they were able to discriminate about the quality of the conferences they chaired? Would they have ideas of what constituted a 'better case conference'? Would they think that child protection conferences were in any way out-moded or did they still find them of value ?

Finding out and the model used

Ideally it would have been better to have attended a conference chaired by the respondents and then interviewed them but unfortunately this was not feasible in every case. One option was to ask questions about attitudes but this might have led only to 'Yes' or 'No' answers or into an expression of theoretical views which would have been difficult to verify with each chairperson. Another option was to place the interview entirely in the hands of the interviewees by asking them how they chaired one of their conferences, but this might produce only a description of the details of that particular case and the particular way they chaired it. It seemed equally important to seek the chairs' responses to specific questions about child protection, as well as their approach to chairing. These two aspects were combined in a guided interview schedule. (See Appendix II.)

Everitt et al (1992) encourage the idea of research which is practitioner influenced and not just researcher led. Practitioners need to share with others 'their theoretical perspectives and assumptions that influence the ways in which they are working' (p. 39). This is not an easy task. They point out that studying people is not like studying a chemical reaction in a test tube. People think and choose and experience feelings, all of which have bearing on what they do. This study combines the two perspectives of a descriptive account of what the chairs did, with what their attitudes and views were in relation to what they did.

The use of the guided interview schedule provided the data from which ideas for the development of a theory or theories would emerge about the way child protection conferences were chaired. Strauss's 'grounded theory' was the model used in the Master of Social Work course at the University of East Anglia and it generated much of the thinking in this study. In particular his guidelines from 'Quality Analysis for Social Scientists' (1987) were used. The guidelines emphasise the complexity of social phenomena and therefore the need for dense theory to account for the wide variation in the phenomena studied.

The small scale sample of fourteen people who chaired conferences lent itself well to this method of exploring personal responses. It was possible to compare and link the self-reported behaviours, the thinking about those behaviours, the general views on abuse and neglect, participation and parenting and the aims and objectives in chairing. There was certainly wide variation in the personalities of the chairpersons, their personal backgrounds, qualifications and life experience but also in the constraints laid upon them by their agencies by virtue of their posts.

The agenda used was one which combined a simple question about how the chairpersons chaired one of their conferences with a number of more complicated questions intended to discover something of their thinking and values by seeking their views on major issues in the field.

The difficulties in the method and some solutions

The temptation to enter into long discussions with the chairpersons on these interesting questions was great but time constraints set boundaries. Only one chairperson retreated into social work jargon making it difficult to discover the meaning of the content of the interview. The other interviews were all laced with a mixture of humour, enthusiasm, ideas, flashes of anger and conviction and reflective insights into the nature of the job. Indeed these chairpersons wanted to talk about this subject.

The initial stage of the interview needed to be focused and uncomplicated so two neutral and factual questions were asked: 'Have you had any training for chairing either within or outside of social services?' and 'Do you prepare in any particular way for a conference?' The next part of the interview focused on the chairing of one particular conference. This was to try and keep the interview rooted in reality. It would have been very easy to float away into theory or fantasy about conferences but by using a specific conference it was possible to relate the questions to a definite event. The chairpersons were asked if they would choose a particular conference they had chaired and use it as a context for their comments. When a visit was arranged for the sole purpose of interviewing the chairperson, the request was made beforehand on the telephone so that s/he would have time to think about it. There were no strictures about which conference. It could be the last one they had chaired, or a particularly difficult one, a particularly easy one, an unusual one or any one! If, however, the writer was visiting the office to observe a child protection conference in her role of researcher for a Department of Health study, the respondent was asked if they would use that conference as their context. This happened in nine out of the fourteen interviews and whilst it did not alter the substance of the interviews it added to the specificity of some of the questions because of the shared experience and allowed for a more equal discussion because both interviewer and interviewee were privy to the same information. Although in the interviews which were linked to conferences which the writer did not attend, there was no means of verifying that the chairperson had chaired them in the way they said they had, there appeared to be no reason to believe that they hadn't. It is useful here to be reminded of the studies of professional judgement (Simmonds in Adcock et al 1991) which indicate a tendency for people from a variety of professions to describe what they do in coming to a judgement markedly differently from what they actually do. In reporting one's actions, one tends to portray them in a better light than may be the fact. But the manner in which the people who chaired the conferences spoke was open. Their accounts seemed genuine because of the detail and clarity in their descriptions and their readiness to share their doubts and uncertainties was striking. In the interviews for the conferences which the writer did attend, it was possible to probe further on the basis of what had been observed. Following the 'take me through the conference' question the chairs were asked for their views on a number of issues, not always in the same order but allowing their responses to lead the questions. Not all the questions, therefore, were included in all the interviews. Spontaneous asides, illustrative examples from other conferences and personal reflections were encouraged because these would act as sidelights to the main spotlight on the subject.

The interviews lasted at least an hour to an hour and a quarter and were taped using a small cassette recorder with TDK D90 audiotapes. Twelve of the interviews were conducted in the offices of the chairpersons and two at the University of East Anglia. It was clearly part of the chairs' job in their role as chairperson to child protection conferences or in their role as team leader or team manager to be constantly available. There was a continual bombardment by others for their advice, information, arrangements or decisions.

The extraneous noises of an ordinary working environment were picked up remarkably clearly on the small recorder, including the shrieks of colleagues' laughter in the next-door offices, intrusive traffic reverberations, the wailing of the wind round the university breeze blocks and other environmental sounds not normally noticed. This assault of the senses in the work setting is not a subject for major comment or attention but it became clear listening to the tapes with great difficulty, what a high level of noise was present and tolerated by the chairpersons whilst they worked.

It might have been fairer to have given notice to the chairs of the questions requiring more thoughtful responses but by not doing so, it was possible to discover whether these issues which would be likely to affect their chairing, were present in their thinking. The readiness of their responses indicated some familiarity of usage, or not. It also revealed whether they had the ability or not, to talk spontaneously about complex subjects and ideas such as would present themselves in conferences and whether they were comfortable with the theories of child abuse and neglect, group-work and decision-making.

Strauss refers (p. 11) to the process in grounded theory analysis of conceiving the theory, elaborating it and checking it. He uses the terms 'induction, deduction and verification.' Original ideas died or developed as the analysis went on. New ideas emerged from listening to the tapes, which developed into richer possibilities for understanding how the chairs chaired. Much of the content of the tapes was transcribed so that comparing and contrasting the replies was made easier. In this way the similar responses were logged into separate blocks and the differences between the blocks noted. Not all the sections lent themselves to this method however. The practicalities of chairing the conferences, for example, were remarkably similar and simply warranted a straightforward description as did some of the other sections. It was interesting to note how common was the practice in chairing in particular areas.

The sample

Fourteen people who chaired conferences from seven different Local Authorities in England agreed to be interviewed. They came from a Northern industrial city, the NSPCC in the Midlands, a new town in the South East, three London Boroughs and a large rural county in the East. There were 10 men and 4 women; the majority were between the ages of 35 and 45: 13 white Europeans and 1 black Afro-Caribbean. Seven were not independent chairs but had direct line management responsibility for the families in the conferences they chaired. They supervised social workers whose cases came to the conferences and they would take responsibility with the social worker for any decisions made about resources or statutory intervention and indeed whether a child protection conference should be held or not. Three others had specialist posts as child care co-ordinators. These posts were independent of the line management of the cases and were used for consultation by team managers and social workers about child abuse and neglect in a variety of ways. The co-ordinators were responsible for developing good practice in child protection and for producing documents and leaflets to enhance this. They were consulted about incidence and severity of abuse and theirs was the final decision about whether to hold a child protection conference. Their status, as defined by salary was above social workers but below team managers. Another three were area officers or equivalent posts. They were responsible for all child care services in the area or district so whilst being two removes away from the client families they were still accountable for the proper delivery of service within the child protection procedures. One other was a team manager who chaired conferences for families from a different team. This seemed an unenviable position to be in, of assessing the working practice of a colleague and another team without the authority within the agency to effect any change which might be necessary. Of the seven team managers chairing their own social workers' cases, only two were strongly against the policy which put them in that position, whereas the others either did not think it mattered particularly or thought there were positive advantages to it.

It was possible to gain easy access to these chairpersons because the researcher was already in contact with them as a result of working on a larger Department of Health funded project 'Family Participation in Child Protection work.' The request was clearly made as a personal one for an hour of their time to talk about the chairing of case conferences. It became necessary to check out with one Local Authority's deputy director that the researcher's approaches were acceptable in terms of using the Local Authority's time and of the respectability of the research itself. Permission was granted readily. The other chairpersons felt able to make the decision about the use of their time themselves and so no negotiations were needed in any other authority.

New ideas from the sample

From this diversity of the chairs' work roles and status came new ideas about what sort of influence the roles and status might have on chairing. Initially it seemed that the influence would be peripheral but increasingly it became clear that, as in Kendrick and Mapstone's work on chairing Child Care Reviews in Scotland it was of significant importance. The decision-making process, particularly about registration, was a far greater problem for the chairs than anticipated and the difference in their methods of dealing with it, was unexpected. The information which arose from talking to the chairpersons about their chosen conference was scrutinized in a variety of ways. By doing this, it was hoped that the influences for their chosen solutions to the decision-making might be discovered. Attempting to interact with all the information on the tapes in order to make these deductions was time consuming but rewarding. By connecting all the different aspects an attempt was made to find possible reasons for their solutions.

For example, the question about managing the conferences produced information about practical aids, organisational methods and then a focus on what was of primary importance to the chairs for their conferences. Intertwined with and influencing their method of dealing with the issues of importance was their individual style of chairing. Then beyond the style, the use of power and beyond that a value system. It would have been possible to view each part of this material as self-contained and leading nowhere in particular. It was only after lengthy consideration of it that ideas began to emerge about the reasons for the way the chairs might be chairing and that their method might be located in their view of who would hold final responsibility for the child protection decisions. This would therefore influence their own part in the management of the case.

Bias in assumptions

Laying down the role of practitioner to be a researcher was a rather long drawn out and painful process. What had already been decided upon from practice and experience was difficult to ditch, even over a period of months, so it was with some reluctance that ideas were discarded. But instead, it is hoped, the chairs and their words have been the source of the deductions and the final guillotine on any personal ideas which did not fit. For example, one bias was that a particular type of personality would be likely to chair easily.

They would be assertive, lucid in their thinking, clear in their language and a touch charismatic. In fact the kind of person one rarely meets. Happily no-one in the study fitted this stereotype, though some of the chairs had some of the characteristics. Whilst some chairs thought they did chair well and others admitted to finding it very difficult, those who had acquired the skills of handling information, people and the unexpected, would be equally capable, whether they thought they could do it well or not. Chairing a child protection conference was a job and like any other, it could be learned and performed but, as they said, it required practice.

A fear, rather than a bias, was that the material would be limited. What could be said of interest from only 14 hours of interviewing? The problem in handling the material was of allowing enough consecutive time to pursue all the ideas that showered from the tapes. The limitations are the writer's.

All the respondents have been given pseudonyms.

8 Training

The people who chaired the conferences had been given little training in preparation for chairing conferences in child protection. Two, on their own initiative, had attended courses for case conference chairs outside their agency, though one described hers as 'backward in its thinking.' Others had received some training in the chairing of meetings generally, on their management courses but it was a brief mention only, not a description of how useful it was, so not likely to have been particularly relevant to child protection conferences. Some had received a half-day in-service training for chairing case conferences at the time of reorganisation and in contrast, all of them had found it helpful. Of the fourteen chairpersons ten had attended a course of some kind though none was enthusiastic about it. Some had chaired meetings in the past outside of social work from which they drew ideas. Most mentioned practical details such as seating, the way to make introductions and of being reminded of issues like 'gossip versus facts,' 'group-speak' and 'hidden agendas' as useful. Four chairs specifically talked of sitting in on colleagues' conferences and learning from them. But no-one had received training for this new type of meeting, called a child protection conference.

Considering the importance of the role of the chair in child protection procedures it is surprising that so little emphasis should have been given to training in this field. What emerged from the replies about training were a number of general points which presented difficulties in chairing and for which training would have been advantageous. There was no mention of training about models of child abuse and neglect, intervention or reaching decisions as might have been expected.

The difficulties of chairing

Bill and Pete reflected on the importance of the whole job, its constant changes and the problems of authority.

> It's such an important job, there's a lot more need for the chairs to be trained because the rules seem to change all the time.

> The whole thing about how to be in authority in the chair and in charge of the meeting and yet use everybody there properly – able to listen and have debates and yet still have some control – these are difficult.

Ivan was categorical about the meeting being chaired as a *business* meeting. He drew from his past experience in plastics technology. Holding a balance between running the business of the meeting and acting as a consultant for the child protection procedures, was, for him, a demanding aspect to chairing. He believed it essential to have someone in the chair experienced and trained in child protection work to provide advice and answers for uncertain professionals from other agencies even though this delayed the progress of the meeting which he found frustrating.

Ben's training in Family Therapy influenced him in his thinking that the conference was a system. He referred to 'working with' the conference much as a therapist would work with a family, a concept very different from the conference as a business meeting, but certainly one that placed him in the enabling role as the chairperson.

Brenda's training had led her to try and distance herself from the conference:

> It's not your meeting. Your job is to accommodate the discussion and direct it.

She had learned this from previous work in a voluntary society where she had observed the paid organiser chair meetings. The use of the word 'direct' suggests the role she used in conferences.

Abe had chaired many meetings in his community work. What he considered important were:

> Communication skills – bringing together professionals and the general public using two sets of communication skills and knowing when people want to speak.

He had become very sensitive to non-verbal communication in case conferences as a result.

Ernest had chaired student meetings in the past and thought the use of language itself contained difficulties.

> You have to look at language – be careful of it.

Bobby regarded aggression and violence as likely to arise in conferences. He found his previous work on these issues in his CQSW course relevant for his chairing.

Pete's previous experience had been in chairing a local political party and a school governors' meeting. He referred to the difficulties of keeping a balance.

> There was politicking and I was still trying to get people to say their bit and get the best out of people and find a balance.

This was useful experience for the chairperson's role of involving all parties in a child protection conference.

Absence of specific training

Social Services had given minimal training to the chairs and they had collected an amalgam of ideas on structure, authority, systems, language and balancing skills from a variety of sources, but there was no clear idea of what was needed to chair a child protection conference. No one mentioned training on the nature, prevalence and incidence of child abuse and neglect. It was as though handling these issues regularly, precluded the need for examining the phenomenon. Risk analysis and how to achieve a decision on registration were not mentioned either. These are the specialised nuts and bolts of chairing child protection conferences and were referred to as problems in other parts of the interviews, yet not one chairperson mentioned a wish for training in them.

It was disconcerting to realise what a limited view had been taken by the agencies of the key position of the chairperson of the conferences. What training they had received was superficial compared with the depth and ramifications of child abuse and neglect. Perhaps even more disconcerting was the acceptance by the chairpersons of their situation. There was an absence of any demand by them for training and no evidence of self-help initiatives. The idea that a chairperson of a child protection conference might need highly specialised training did not emerge from the tapes. On the contrary, most of the interviewees seemed to indicate that it was one task among many for which they were responsible and which they carried out as best they could.

9 Preparation

'I like to go into a conference with a clean mind,' was the answer of one respondent to the question, 'Do you prepare for case conferences?' He was line manager for the cases which came to his conferences and so knew all the issues concerning the families. He went on to explain the importance for him of *'hearing* what other people have to say,' suggesting his need to clear his mind of previous ideas gained from prior knowledge of the family in order to fully comprehend the information. He needed to distance himself from his team manager role whilst he was in the role of the chair to the conference. He regarded an attempt to achieve neutrality as part of his preparation but was it possible?

This was one of a wide variety of ways in which the chairs prepared themselves.

Details of the case

All except one of the people who chaired the conferences prepared to some degree by familiarising themselves with the details of the case. The extent to which they did this varied from looking at the file notes to a concentrated discussion with the social worker.

Bobby was the only chairperson who made a point of *not* looking at the file nor of talking to the social worker.

> I find it a handicap.

George looked at files but did not usually talk to social workers

> ... because they tend to want to clarify everything that will go through – I don't find that helpful. I say to them 'Come in with differing views'.

Six of the other chairs had discussions beforehand which might include talking to parents. Maude said,

> Sometimes it's very closely scripted, especially if it's very complicated.

Brenda sat down with the new social workers in her team though 'not with the Level IIIs' and prepared with them and expected them to write a report for the conference.

Greg said,

> I'll look the week beforehand at all case conferences and see whether they're complicated i.e. the nature of the incidents or whether the child was previously registered or if it's a transfer and then go through those papers. If it's complex I'd contact the social worker or team leader to see if there'd be any particular difficulties.

The underlying question about preparation is whether, when parents attend, the conference is stage-managed to avoid conflict. A chairperson would be foolish not to take account of controversial issues in relation to the family but making plans regarding the decision-making would be patently inconsistent with the notion of neutrality.

Penny and Bill both liked to get 'a flavour' of the case by reading the file. For Bill this was,

> ... to work through in my head various possible ways the conference could go so that when the real thing occurs you've gone through some of the debate.

This strategy of considering alternatives beforehand, ready to offer to the conference, accords well with one of the aspects of competent group functioning in the literature.

Greg referred similarly to

> ... looking at realistic options. I do it (list the options) to be clear what the issues will be so we don't get fudged or blurred issues.

Neutrality

As well as the chairperson quoted at the beginning of this section, eight others indicated in their responses to the question about preparation that they had considered the notion of neutrality. It was clearly an issue which concerned them in relation to how they prepared. There were two entirely different approaches neither of which, contrary to expectation, exactly reflected their positions in line management. The line managers seemed to be more anxious about neutrality in that they mentioned it more frequently as a problem. They struggled with their close involvement with the cases, to gain clarity and not to make their minds up beforehand, whereas the non-line managers either chose to have no prior knowledge or by contrast, very detailed knowledge. They used both of these bases to enhance their control of the chairing. The mental gymnastics used to clear the mind of previous knowledge were not convincing as a method of achieving neutrality and the alternatives seemed to sway between a view that a little knowledge of the case was allowable beforehand to help the process along, and a view that it was very much in the interests of the conference for the chairperson to know what it was all about, especially if the case was complex. There seems to be a confusion here about what kind of details should be known beforehand by the chairperson so as to be informed but not to jeopardise neutrality.

Jim (not an immediate line manager) described getting the social worker and team leader together

> to look at what has happened and what they're thinking and try and separate out the case work stuff from the child protection parts. What I like to do is keep the casework out of them because it can become not murky but foggy! Other people can try to set the casework framework. The conference is about *child protection* and what all the agencies can put into practice to *protect* that child.

Penny's approach (not a line manager) was that she would decide what issues she wanted information on:

> I read the file and give the team manager some ideas about what I would be looking at.

Abe (a line manager) said,

> What I don't want to do is to go into a case conference with one point of view already resolved.

and Ernest,

> The problem of being a line manager is not to have formulated the decision before you've got your basic information.

Whilst not referring to the neutrality issue directly most of the chairs seemed aware of it and referred to it indirectly in their approaches to the conferences. Either they wanted to run the conference with clarity because it was complex and therefore they chose to be closely involved in prior discussions or they wished to be separate from too much discussion and therefore would allow themselves only a flavour of it.

Ben's (also a line manager) concern for the 'clean mind' illustrated the same anxiety. Herein is the difficulty. Where details of factual information are sought, the conference is enabled to proceed quicker but if in doing so, discussion of social work plans influences the way the conference makes its decision then neutrality is compromised. What occurred seemed to depend on the importance to the chairperson of having a grasp of the complexity of the case.

Other professionals being present and prepared

All the respondents were agreed upon the importance of getting the right people to the conference. They felt that if this was not achieved then the information made available to the conference would be deficient and therefore the decisions to protect the child would not be satisfactory.

> I'd decide beforehand who would be helpful to the conference. There are occasions when its important to have expertise to help people make judgements and I think it's the responsibility of the chair to see they are there.

> I knew I'd have to cross the bridge of legal decision-making (in a neglect case) so I was keen to have a solicitor there.

The chairs were unanimous also in expecting other professional workers to be prepared.

> I hate it when people are not prepared. I'd challenge afterwards. I have sympathy if the case conference is short notice but I get cheesed off with people who don't prepare.

> I expect people to come prepared with a very clear analysis and a very clear view. If someone is really unprepared I'd see them afterwards. If the key-worker can't be clear what the issues are – what about the child?

> I like them to come prepared and I say 'make sure your contribution is relevant, factual and clear'.

Penny relied on the team managers in her area to ensure their social workers prepared a written report for the conference.

What influenced preparation?

What the chairperson did about preparation appeared to depend on their personal view of what was more important – trying to be neutral or knowing sufficient information beforehand to manage legal or social work issues. They might therefore do nothing and try and keep themselves ignorant of the kind of case it might be or they might know the issues as a line manager and try to erase them from their minds or they might thrash out complex issues first with the social worker and the team leader. These stances appeared to relate to their status and power within social services and this will be returned to later in the next chapter. There was evidence that some useful chairing skills were being practised in thinking through options and possibilities and in seeking further information and the keenness to have all the evidence 'on the table' but these did not emerge as a corporate view.

The non-line managers who prepared according to the complexity of the case and were willing to challenge what they considered less then good contributions from other people were the chairs who appeared to be confidently independent in their role. They did not hold case responsibility and their independence appeared to enable them to use their own standards to discriminate about severity and complexity as well as about standards of presentation.

There was little mention of practical preparation of the room, nor of the need for the chairperson to prepare parents for the conference. If the chairs were taking seriously the notion that *all* members of the conference were responsible for the task in hand, then I would have expected them to have been more active in ensuring that the *whole* of the conference was prepared, not just themselves, but this was not evident.

10 Managing the conference

In practical and organisational ways, the management of the conference was described remarkably similarly by all the chairs but their methods of management appeared to reflect their different views of what they perceived as priority and of importance in their conferences.

I had not formally observed the conferences they chaired in relation to their chairing so I had no substantiated means of knowing whether they did what they said they did, even though I had attended nine conferences of the fourteen chairs in another capacity. They might have been describing the official guidelines in their own words for me but, I have to say, that their descriptions were considerably more individualistic than any guidelines and sufficiently realistic in not painting too rosy a picture of their chairing, to persuade me of their validity and that, overall, they were probably describing what they actually did though it has to be remembered that there are a number of studies which suggest that reported behaviour differs from actual behaviour, particularly in relation to professional judgement (Simmonds, in Adcock et al 1991).

Practical aids to the conference

Some of the people who chaired conferences used practical aids such as agendas, the Area Child Protection Committee Handbook for reference, printed categories of abuse available for every member of the conference, pen and paper for parents to use, notebooks for themselves. They also used a verbal preface to each conference which was a statement usually about confidentiality and then the names, addresses, dates of birth of family members. This would forestall situations where professionals found themselves in the wrong conference and it also set a suitably serious note to the start of the proceedings.

Most chairs used a chronological order or logical sequence in the presentation of the information to the conference. In the main this consisted of: introductions, incident, family background, risk assessment, registration and protection plan. Bill referred to this as 'chunking' the conference into sections and Pete as 'making discrete parcels.' Bill said at various points he would summarise. He did this to manage anxiety because it was the way he found he could 'keep control.' Six of the other chairs adopted these two methods of sectioning the conference and summarising.

Organising the conference

The question, 'Can you take me through how you chaired this conference?' brought out two main concerns: one was to gain all the relevant information and the other to reach the decision leading to registration. In pursuit of these two ends the issue of control or 'being in charge' emerged as a theme in their replies. There were several references to 'keeping them on track,' to 'keeping control' and to the necessity of 'bringing them back to the protection of the child.' The chairs were highly conscious of the importance of being in charge of the conference. To do this they used not only their skills but power, either personal power or the power invested in the role of the chair which for many was linked to and derived from their status in social services' hierarchy, or both. The point at which they used their power depended on what they regarded as a priority or of importance for the conference.

Priorities for the chairs

> I go for the straight facts and then I try and see the opinions and emotions around and what are the likely outcomes for the protection of the child. I say, 'Does anyone feel this child is at risk? What changes need to occur to reduce the levels of anxiety – what do people feel needs to happen?'

These comments go straight to the point of protection and could be construed as the chair's first concern being the child's protection. Looked at in a slightly different way, it is a curious question to ask because it suggests that if the professionals are *not* anxious, then the child will not be at risk. Relieving the professionals' anxiety levels may not necessarily be the way to protect a child. It does not take account of high personal levels of anxiety which might lead to over-cautious management nor low levels which may prevent accurate risk analysis.

Eliciting all the relevant information was a priority for George and Maude and affected the way their conferences started. They were emphatic about the importance of including all participants and they both went out of their way to set the scene at the start to indicate the significance of everyone's contribution.

> My function is to ensure you all have your say.
>
> I make sure everyone who is there has a chance to contribute because the person who can easily get missed out can have the most important information.

George went on to illustrate this with his example conference where the mother was suffering from mental illness and it was the lowest status nurse in the conference who had the closest observation of her on a daily basis on the ward.

Maude's reasons for giving time and thought to the way the beginning of the conference was conducted were because she wanted to make the conference:

> open and creative and allow for the emotional bits rather than behave in an authoritarian manner and not allow people their say because it's *your* agenda and you're sticking to it.
>
> You need to work really hard at the beginning – the manner in which you greet people, set out the agenda and the process and begin to conduct it ...

Bobby had strong views about taking the incident as priority before the family background because he felt it allowed for an expression of stored emotion about the case.

> People (need) to unblock about the investigation and incident. The health visitor and social worker carry a lot of feelings – 'how I was responsible' and yet they have to deal factually with the incident.

A number of chairs referred to 'getting the facts out.' They regarded these as significant for decision-making. Nancy said that if the facts dictated the course of action there would be no problems about decisions, but if they did not, the other professionals would distance themselves from a decision, as in the context case she used as her example. The abuse had occurred to a 7 year-old boy at school. The facts which were presented, were injuries to the boy's scrotum. They were diagnosed differently by two consultant paediatricians – one diagnosing physical abuse and the other sexual abuse. In this case the facts were not sufficient to dictate the course of action because they were interpreted in two different ways. There was no clear or satisfactory explanation. The mother had already taken steps to protect her son by removing him from the school where the abuse had taken place. In her view this removed him from any further abuse. The conference was one I attended and it floundered about whether to register him or not.

Nancy commented

> Sometimes people see facts in their heads but it isn't in what they say, so I try and get them to state the obvious even when it sends someone out of the room.

This is what happened to the young class-teacher in the case. She did not want to see the police photographs of the abuse and left the room having heard the medical description before the photographs were circulated. The professionals could not arrive at a decision about registration and Nancy herself made the decision to register. It went unchallenged by the professionals and only the mother protested afterwards when she was called in to hear the conclusions. She felt registration was pointless in the circumstances because she had taken steps already to protect her child.

In this situation Nancy chose not to challenge the conference to think through whether to register or not but to make the decision herself in her role as chairperson. Her formula of relying on the facts to dictate the action did not facilitate the decision about registration and in the dilemma, she used her power as the chairperson to decide.

Penny stepped in, in one of her conferences with her knowledge and expertise as a Child Abuse specialist to protect a child where the social worker had said she thought access to the child by the abuser was acceptable.

> I took over because I didn't think that was good enough and I said so. I didn't want the conference influenced by that – it wasn't OK for this man to be visiting. I couldn't allow that view to dominate the conference – that would have been very wrong.

Here was an example of the chairperson outside of the line management acting unilaterally on an issue related to the alleged abuse by influencing the conference with her own views. She did not give the conference the opportunity to consider the rights of the alleged abuser in this instance, nor did she offer the access issue to the conference for debate as part of the protection plan. She influenced the conference strongly at this point on the basis of her own expertise and knowledge. The people who chair conferences accumulate much practice wisdom about local levels of child abuse and therefore from the point of view of experience, their contribution is important. However such contributions should be subject to the same scrutiny and substantiation as other contributions so the chairs should share their information with the conference as they expect other members to do.

George used his role to control the timing of the conference strictly because he found difficulties in

> ... getting it how you want it – not enough time.

Brenda had as her priority 'setting the scene' of the conference by outlining the way she would take information, 'because that sets it for me' so that 'I start to tease out.' In setting her framework for the conference she gathered the material she wanted for decision-making but her discussion went on to indicate that the final decision was hers. The 'teasing out' was not shared with the conference.

Despite these clear responses about what was important and what was priority, the chairs still had problems in putting them into practice.

...tting the conference to work as a group

Abe thought the difficult part was:

> ... actually saying to the conference the summary of the issues and encouraging them to see it's *not* my decision. It's a *conference* decision and *they* accept responsibility ...

> You have to say this is a conference decision and it belongs to everyone.

Other chairs echoed this difficulty:

> I am always putting the responsibility on the conference and enabling the conference as whole to come to a decision.

> It's *our* decision (i.e. the conference's). I feel quite strongly about that. I'm always putting things back to the conference.

Three of the chairs mentioned aspects of the conference in terms of group behaviour suggesting that group theory was part of their thinking and part of the way they tried to understand the conferences.

> It needs certain types of personalities to make the group effective. A group will influence an individual, and a group when faced with anxiety can do quite radical things. I've known conferences worry and come up with *very* odd decisions.

> It was obvious that the group (the conference) was of like mind about their views on the level of neglect in the family. I felt that by bringing it all round together that it was important then not to pussy-foot about because of the general agreement about the neglect. Sometimes with a regular group there's a danger of familiarity but I'm aware of that.

> There are group processes coming into play here. The concentration span of the working group is 40-50 minutes, so past an hour you get a sense of those who have spoken and have lost it, so I try and speed things up, especially if there's a lot of information.

These references place at least some of the chairing within the structure of a specific theory being used by the chairs but these were isolated examples. There were few other references to a conceptual framework for thinking about the conferences.

2) Challenging the members and maintaining control

Using challenging behaviour in order to gain information and make decisions was described by a number of chairpersons, though they did not find it easy:

> I couldn't let that go without challenging it.
>
> I'm always saying 'Do you really think that?' and challenging them.
>
> I try to be very specific about what has happened because the conference has to be clear about future risk to the child – a bit more legalistic.

Achieving a balance of being in control without being directive presented problems. Pete illustrated this in the neglect case he used as his context example.

> I just had to dive in without trying to be directive and try to get the group to give you the decision rather than you give them ... but ... with neglect, the level at which you can arbitrate and talk about it is not a unitary level – there's no way you can fix it. The level of household neglect could be an impending disaster but this one, because of the family, you have to measure it against cultural norms.

This was another conference I observed and although as a cultural issue the neglect was referred to obliquely, it was not defined as such when considering registration and the protection plan for the child. An open contribution at that point from the chair about what constituted neglect for the purpose of the conference might have enabled the conference to make a more informed decision through discussion of their views, rather than Pete's intervention from the chair. Here was an example of a line manager not offering the issue to the conference for discussion.

Bill, by contrast cut through the problems by being frankly directive:

> I'd identify what I assess to be the most important areas of concern or areas needing further investigation and summarise and ask if anyone wants to add (anything) and then I make my decisions and recommendations.

He confessed to thoroughly enjoying that kind of 'crystallised social work assessment' in the conference.

> When I go into a conference only with the bare bones, my main task is assessing just exactly what has been said and thinking on your feet and juggling it all around so that you're in a position to make some of the decisions for the recommendations at the end. I see that process as the single most important thing for me.

3) *Legal decisions and the presence of lawyers in conferences*

Decisions about the immediate safety of the child would have to be made before the conference but some of the chairs used the conference later to gather more evidence for Care proceedings. They might ask the local authority solicitor to be present to test whether the evidence would stand up in court. The presence of a solicitor in the conference may be using the conference as a short-cut to the social work decision about whether the protection of the child requires legal proceedings and there is some debate as to whether a child protection conference can be the best place for that decision to be made in any case (Owen 1991). The conference may recommend but should not make that decision. Other problems are also introduced if a lawyer is present at the same time as parents and the question has to be asked whether it is more important for parents to be present or lawyers? (Thoburn 1992) In some authorities the solicitor's role is confined to that of an observer.

> Usually a decision about protection has already been made earlier. There has to be a decision at the time of the investigation. The majority of conferences we have lead to a discussion of legal proceedings.

> It's a corporate response. There have been occasions when it's been necessary to tackle care as a response to the protection issue, so I'd have the legal representative at the conference.

4) Abuse by the system

Maude outlined another problem. For her, the protection of the child was weakened by the unknown outcome of the conference. This caused her sadness and frustration especially in cases of alleged sexual abuse when she said she knew that:

> The way the systems are set up, they are not helpful. I find that *really* hard. Neither the legal nor the care system can cope and the reality is that these children don't want to see their uncles or fathers taken away. What they want is the abuse to stop. What we end up doing is ... dismembering the family and with very little skill to put it back together again.

Her far-sightedness about the case-work implications was present in her thinking whilst she was chairing the conference. To what extent this affected her chairing or the outcome of the conference is, of course, difficult to assess, but as a response to chairing a conference, it was a sudden spotlight into her anguish for the child, whose well-being would be affected by the conference decision and the abuse perpetrated by the system.

5) Taking responsibility for the recommendations

Jim was only too aware of the limitations of the system.

> There has to be some clear boundaries when it comes to responsibility.

He was referring not only to the performance of other professionals but also to the lack of experience and pressure of work on his own social workers who might be unable to fulfil what was asked of them.

Ivan was prepared as a last resort to make the decisions himself in the conference but the protection plan he thought should remain with the social worker or indeed, if the parents were present, with them.

The best decisions about protection are often made by the parents.

6) Issues of cultural difference and gender

A question asked in a few of the interviews was whether the chairs had encountered issues of race or gender in their conferences and what they had done in response. These arose from discussion about how the chairs tried to keep control. Jim, the only black respondent, spoke spontaneously about the issue and the problems it presented.

> The society where I come from, physical chastisement was the thing. There was no talking to children. People where I come from use physical chastisement.

His black social workers would say to him, 'Ah ... you're not going to conference that are you – because that's (physical punishment) what we do?' He found himself having to question his staff about what was acceptable parenting.

> Well – is it? Is it what we do and how appropriate is it? You've got to come to me with an assessment of *that* family situation before coming out with general statements like that. It might be what we *did* but it's not what we do in the present.

He was taking a firm line on the boundary of intervention, based on his current experience as a chairperson, his own standards of parenting, his social work values and his cultural differences, none of which was easy for his chairing role. The fact that he came from an ethnic minority and was readily challenged by social workers from the same cultural background, brought into focus more clearly than for the other chairs I interviewed, the way in which members of their conferences would use their own personal and cultural value systems to make judgements about parenting.

Penny thought that overt racism was a more straightforward problem to deal with. Her local authority had a publicly-stated anti-racist policy which was displayed in all the offices and she had been able to deal with outright racist remarks easily. She thought gender issues were much more subtle to have to deal with. She had detected a tendency to get information about women and mothers in her conferences that she did not get about men, with regard to sexual relationships. She found that men got more sympathy if they were on their own looking after children and that the professionals took a 'wider and less judgemental view' of them and were prepared to offer more resources than for women in similar situations. 'Women are supposed to be more caring and there are very high demands made on them.'

Nancy had to take a general practitioner to task for what she regarded as a sexist remark he made. The discussion was in connection with the alleged sexual abuse of the daughter and whether the mother was aware of it. Because the mother worked as a 'kissogram' employee, he said, 'Oh, well, what do you expect from a mother like that.' Nancy said she had to point out that the two were not necessarily related.

These examples were given as the sort of problems which arose in conferences even when the chairs had well worked out priorities in chairing. The element of surprise as well as the tactical difficulties in dealing with such remarks required quick thinking and tactful language.

The end of the conference

The same problems in group decision-making were encountered and accentuated when it came to registration and the protection plan. Registration is the one decision the conference has to make. Some chairs made a direct recommendation about it:

> I do say, 'I think we should register.'

> My mind is going over all the ins and outs being mindful of our criteria and I would then say 'It's my understanding and recommendation that registration should take place.'

> In view of ... etc., my feeling is towards registration.

> There are times when I think the case conference is mad. They can be mad – neurotic and anti-work. If I feel this is happening, the chair is the only person who is sane and must stay with the hard facts and decide.

> I think it's happened and we should register.

> I do say what I think – try not to be too forceful about it.

and those who took a consensus,

> I will go back to the debate if necessary and ask 'What are your objections, your concerns?'

> I sum up and say, 'It looks to me as though we have three options. We have said this, or this, or this.' I give alternatives of what we could do.

> I don't think it is for the chair to decide. I say 'This is my understanding of what we have; these are the grounds for registration,' and on the basis of that, ask them to respond spontaneously. I don't go round and say 'Do you agree, do you agree' – I'm not taking an AGM. I'm trying to get a major decision in relation to that child and family and the work to be done.

> We have difficulties here. Let's go back over it again because it's important that the conference makes a judgement.
>
> I try and achieve a consensus ... Are you happy to go along?

Ben said, if in a dilemma about consensus,

> I'll take a majority view and minute the minority.

Penny and Bobby both volunteered that the problems about registration as far as they were concerned were not with the regular conference members but

> with the teachers and school attenders and the voluntary agencies who don't really understand what the register is about.
>
> It is easy to use your authority to guide them through.
>
> They regard it as a belt and braces but it's used really to protect themselves.

Maude was the chairperson who spontaneously said she did not think registration was useful.

> It appears a nice safety mechanism but what does it achieve?

Given that there may be a tendency in the conference to err on the side of caution rather than risk (Evans 1990, Gibb 1989), the chairperson needs to use the decision-making techniques skilfully at this juncture so that the conference is not unduly influenced by members whose experience and knowledge is limited. Also, when parents are present, even if, as in some conferences, they are not allowed to take part in the decision, the chairperson needs to take account of the effect that parents might have in the conference which would lead the conference to caution. If parents have not been well prepared they may let themselves down in the conference through nervousness, with behaviour likely to produce doubt on the part of the professionals or 'proof' of their lack of parenting abilities and might influence the conference towards a 'belt and braces' type of registration. The chairperson needs to preserve the balanced view.

Penny's tactic was to ask the team leader first:

> I'd always start with the social work manager. Ideally you don't want the team manager and social worker to disagree. One reason to ask the manager is it shifts it off the social worker – the family can see the social worker as part of the agency. The onus is shifted to the conference and not the individual social worker.

There is real divergence here about how the chairs dealt with the problems of managing the meeting. On the one hand there was a substantial group anxious that the conference made group decisions, but at the same time uncertain about their own role as chairs in how to persuade colleagues to do this. On the other, a group who either decided for the conference, or had virtually decided before the conference began.

A distinct tension is illustrated in the descriptions between the planned practical measures and intentions of the chairs, and the means they would use to carry out their intentions of gaining information, so that decisions and recommendations could be made. It resolved itself in two styles of chairing. There were those who like sheep-dogs rounded up the flock and made a group decision and those who like the Pied Piper marched cheerfully ahead and made the decision alone, hoping the members would continue to follow. A definition of each style might be 'authoritarian' and 'participatory'. Of the fourteen people who chaired the conferences, I would allocate seven to the 'participatory' category and four to the authoritarian category with three in a category where they chaired 'participatively' for most of the conference but at the point of registration jumped to the 'authoritarian' style. These methods of chairing, which emerged from this section on managing the conferences, will be analysed further in the next section in connection with style, power and status.

Advocates or apologists?

Another difference in the way the conferences were managed appeared to reflect the views of the chairs about their own power as the chairperson or the power of the social services agency in the case. One definition might be 'the advocate for the child' and the other 'the apologist for the agency.' The 'advocates for the child' were prepared to distance themselves, to a degree, from social services as an agency and from taking on responsibility as the chairperson for the decisions of the conference. The 'apologists', on the other hand, remained involved in their social services role, appearing to use the conference as a back-up either to decisions already made or as an extension to the task of their own agency.

Of the 'advocates' group, six of the seven had no line management for the case, whereas in the 'apologists' group six of the seven had immediate line management for the case they were conferencing. This might have been expected and appeared to be evidence of the difficulties of remaining neutral. Where the chairs were independent of the case they appeared to find it easier to use their power in the role of the chair overtly on behalf of the child in order to achieve an inter-disciplinary decision in the conference and occasionally by their interventions, sometimes to the point of jeopardising the ability of the conference to participate in decision-making. Where they were line managers they appeared to use their social services agency power in an undeclared way, defending the agency or acting on its behalf.

The responses about the protection plan stage of the conferences, were interestingly not about protection as such, but about multi-agency working. Many positive views emerged:

> It's really important to have an understanding of each other for the plan and to have informal meetings as well, talking things through, letting off steam because we do come into conflict from time to time and we can sit down and talk it through.
>
> In the bit about helping the family there is a discrete task for each agency and I say 'Are you able to carry that out?'
>
> There's a lot of clout when you come back and you haven't done it.
>
> It's better to have a multi-agency forum for the discussion of the plan. It does mean there is a focus and check on things, that there wouldn't be otherwise and without a chair you wouldn't get that.
>
> The different disciplines do their bit and you get a variety of opinion and understandings and they do take the plan seriously.
>
> Understanding between parties has improved because of the disasters and the Guidelines and working out the recommendation and through clearer understanding of our tasks and the understanding that some agencies have to specialise in particular areas of the plan.
>
> Because representatives of all agencies are there, there's ownership (of the protection plan) by the whole and this invests it with greater authority than if it was only one agency – greater authority than if it was just a case discussion.

These quotations provide a vigorous argument for continuing to involve all the agencies in the plan despite difficulties, and an appreciation of the importance and value of each fulfilling their role in it. There is also a hint that because the plan is a multi-agency sharing of responsibility, there are fewer difficulties for the chairperson in facilitating it. Ten years after Hallett and Stevenson's examination of inter-agency co-operation (1980) when they found that different agency reactions were an impediment to decision-making, these professionals spoke more positively of the multi-disciplinary dynamics of the conferences.

However it is surprising that there was little discussion of the nature of the protection plans and whether they could be adequately composed in the conference. Baglow (1990) has suggested that 'the appropriate treatment package to choose is particularly likely to be overlooked' (p. 392) because long-term plans do not engage members in the same way as the discussion of the crisis intervention.

11 Style, power and status

There were no questions about style in the schedule but nevertheless an indication of the style of each chairperson emerged during the interview. My reminder, 'but tell me *how* you did it' elicited not only practical examples of chairing tactics and skills but also self-portraits.

For example three chairs spoke of themselves as 'tight,' 'tenacious' and 'no nonsense' in their approach. In order to achieve that approach they set what might be called 'elephant traps' for conference members. They would say to a member,

> If we go to Court, would you be saying that in the witness box?

and

> I'll use techniques to count out those with no direct involvement with the family and I'll say 'What I want to do now is to pick up on what the family is like' and ignore the others.

and

> I might insist very nicely that someone explains and I suggest 'I'm a bit confused. What research has led you to that conclusion?'

and

> You really don't believe that, do you?

or

> I try and make people at ease so I make sure that the conference is not a ventilation – no antagonism or animosity.

Here are descriptions of directive and sometimes abrasive chairing styles. These chairs regarded themselves as successful in chairing.

> I think I'm quite good at chairing.
>
> I'm clear I have the ability to chair.
>
> I think I'm very good at letting everyone have their say. Someone gives you a stroke and says 'I like coming to your conferences.'

The other chairs were more tentative about themselves. They used phrases such as: 'open and honest,' 'collaborative,' 'being clear,' 'finding a balance,' 'moving things on,' 'a participatory kind of person,' and aimed at achieving their approach by using 'listening skills,' 'drawing out everything that's there,' 'asking them leading questions,' 'asking for help in summarising,' 'conducting and orchestrating,' and 'spotting the ones (conference members) who can't act as responsibly and knowledgeably as you.'

These responses describe chairing in a way more akin to traditional social work skills of accurate empathy, warmth and genuineness, honesty and listening and responding. These chairs' view of themselves was more uncertain than the first group but ranged from two who enjoyed the job, through to those who could not say they actually liked it:

> I always get stage-fright,

to those who found it difficult:

> It is a difficult task and I'm still working on it.
>
> It's not my first love.

However, they were not namby-pamby in their approach to things which they might consider to be out of order in their conferences.

> I try to be tactful if they are making outrageous statements. I'll press them gently to justify their statements.
>
> I'd say in the nicest possible way, if you have people talking together 'Could you say that to all of us?'
>
> People say to me, 'Do you choose not to hear it or do you address it?' Now I always choose to address it because if you don't do that it always comes back. It has to be tackled.
>
> I try and knock it on the head in the most diplomatic way.
>
> I'd say, 'We have to have very specific information and unless it's something we've heard ourselves then I don't think we can regard it.'

Managing the other professionals in the conference so that information could be shared competently, seemed to be attempted in two different styles: a 'barrister' style and a 'social work' style. Both included clarity about dealing with unacceptable remarks but appeared to be different in expression. The difference might be found in the tone of the questioning and reflect a controlling use of the role of the chair leading to distancing between chairperson and members of the conference. This use of the controlling aspect of the role in one part of the conference would not lend itself later to corporate decision-making about registration. Human nature being what it is, members of the conference may well resist further open comments if they have already been publicly reprimanded.

Relating this to the method of decision-making in the section on management, chairs were divided differently within the 'barrister'/'social work' groups, into those who strove to make it a conference decision, – the 'sheepdogs', and those who made the decision themselves as the chair, – the 'Pied Pipers' and those who might suddenly change from being the 'sheepdogs' to being the 'Pied Pipers'. There seemed to be no connection, as might be expected between 'barrister' style and 'Pied Pipers', and 'social worker' style and 'sheepdogs.' To account for this, gender was considered as a possible factor. Feminist writers in social work and in social work research describe distinct methods and styles which women use in their work which are allied to personal gentleness and sensitivity. (Kelly (1988) and Dominelli and McLeod (1989). Pottage and Evans (1992) in a study of work-based stress allude to the need to develop a more co-operative operating style as compared to a competitive masculine method of management. They comment that women prefer to use personal power whereas men rely on positional power (p. 19). In this study the issue of gender did not appear to include the chairs' methods as two of the four women used an 'authoritarian' method and two a 'participatory' method in decision-making.

In considering whether personality or even lack of time might account for the way chairs adopted their particular method and style of chairing there appeared to be no likely reasons for this but a possible reason for chairs adopting an 'authoritarian' method to chair their conferences may be as a response to stress. Pottage and Evans (1992) list a number of situations which social workers cannot avoid (p. 24) which subtly trap them, eating away at self esteem and self image. Conferences encapsulate some of these situations. 'There is tension between individual professional values and goals of caring, and meeting the needs of the organisation' (p. 28). In conferences, 'authoritarian' decision-making or a 'barrister' style is one way of meeting the organisation requirement to decide about registration and to control the process.

Whichever style a chairperson adopts it should be consistent whether authoritarian or participatory. Conference members need to know where they are in relation to it, especially if it changes. There was no evidence of such understanding being conveyed by the chairperson to the conference members. These differences in chairing style reflect similar styles advocated in social work training which enable social workers to operate participatively in certain situations and to use authority in others.

The literature search yielded ideas from Kendrick and Mapstone's work on chairing child care reviews in Scotland about the effect of status on chairing (1989) and so a specific question about the power of the chairperson in relation to their status as a manager (and for the NSPCC chairperson, their independent status) was included in the interviews.

This question produced responses on the personal nature of power and the power of the agency. Most of the chairs sat uneasily and uncertainly between these two sources of their authority. The NSPCC chairperson was an exception, and spoke with a wicked twinkle in his eye about being able to challenge 'any suspicion of a cosy Social Services line.' He described the NSPCC needing to recruit social workers as chairs who had 'a lot of bottle' and 'confidence' implying that these were qualities which in his view were useful to the chairing task. He reaffirmed that the meeting was his:

> It's *my* meeting,

indicating his independence and control of it.

Another chairperson who led his conferences from the front, described how he frequently engaged in,

> long and fraught discussions with members from other agencies who have felt that what I have said, despite the backing of the team leader and the social worker, was unacceptable to them and then I find I'm duty bound to explain our (SSD) philosophy and how we see our relationship with the individual client and that no matter what decision is made we ought to be able to convey to the client that decision and be able to continue to work with them.

His comment was in connection with matters of confidentiality and what could be shared with families. He thus moved swiftly in these situations from the neutral chair to become the spokesperson for the Social Services in order to defend his social workers against other professionals' expectations of them. His view of exerting power via the status of his role was expressed in terms of justifying to the members of the conference the tough decisions which might give his social workers a hard time. He said,

> I wouldn't ask a member of my staff to do something without supporting them.

When a confrontational situation arose in his conferences he would play his role as manager for Social Services.

There were three other chairs who spoke about using power to defend the Social Services Department. They were uncomfortable with it.

> I've had to deal with attacks because the chair was seen as a defender of the Social Services. The chair has responsibility to remain impartial. It's difficult.

> I've certainly felt at times that I could make the conference go the way I wanted. I have to be very careful of it. I feel I represent the Department's position.

> There's a lot of power in the chair. I don't know how you get round that. I do say what I think but try not to be too forceful about it. The most difficult bits are when there are hidden agendas between professionals and there are many of those.

This question about power produced replies about the chairs' role as managers in Social Services and their discomfort in trying to defend their department whilst trying to keep neutrality as the chair and it raised the question as to whether it was really possible for them to retain neutrality throughout a conference.

However, the same question to Nancy prompted the reply that she saw her power deriving from her personal authority. She thought that her role as chair was powerful because the conference members accepted her leadership.

> It is a powerful role and a powerful place to be in. I don't know how it's viewed by others. You earn your ticket.

Here she allied the power to the quality of her chairing but she did give an example against herself illustrating how her leadership powers were challenged by her own social worker who disagreed with her. Nancy had to compromise and record the difference of opinion in the minutes. She reflected that either one or the other of these two approaches had to be right. It troubled her that she did not know whether it was her approach as chair or the social worker's. Her stated belief in her impartiality in gaining a *conference* decision actually receded when her leadership was challenged especially by someone below her in power in the agency. The way she dealt with it was not to seek further information and clarification from the conference but to accept the two opposing views as alternatives and take a majority vote from the chair which would re-establish her leadership role in the meeting. Had she attempted to marry the two views, by asking for more information, there might have been a better chance of a genuine conference decision.

Ben's view was also that power was focused in his personal authority.

> It's not misusing the power of the chair but making it enabling, by bringing in research findings. I say there are some predisposing factors the conference might like to consider.

He thought the chair's role was:

> one of earned respect for the person not purely status.

The remaining group who responded to the question minimised the power of the chair altogether:

> It's not so important as people make out. It's back to personal responsibility in chairing.

Ivan felt that it was just a job to be carried out as well as possible, like any other within his brief.

> The chair doesn't have any power of its own. It's dependent on the power that other people ascribe to it and whether the level of expertise is recognised. It's actually a very weak position. The chair has power over only one decision in the Child Protection plan and that is registration.

Ernest explained that despite any case conference recommendations, the area office might override the case conference. He put his finger directly on the lack of any executive power vested in the conferences. Nevertheless it should be pointed out that a conference can decide that it believes the child has or has not been abused. It can also stick a very powerful label on a family which may be, and often is, used in Court. The decision to register a child may have consequences for good or ill for that child. He thought that any personal authority of the chair was ascribed by others as a result of the chairperson having developed a skill in the role. He also saw his own power resting on his chairing skills, not implicit in the role itself, nor in the person but rather in the performance.

Finally, a comment by Jim raised an interesting possibility.

> I think sometimes if you weren't aware of the importance of keeping the balance of the power then someone ought to be monitoring your process in that.

He suggested that chairs should be inspected to see if they were being objective, fair and just. He went on,

> It would be ridiculous not to acknowledge that there is a lot of power in the chair. I've not had it challenged because I give people the opportunity to voice their views and I pose questions and try not to make statements.

In trying to locate the source of the chairs' power there were indications from their responses in attributing it to either their Social Services role or to their personal characteristics. If the role of the chairperson were to be truly independent then a chairperson would be able to develop a style using the power in the role explicitly, either authoritatively or participatively but for most of the respondents, there was confusion about whether the power lay in the status, line management or employment by social services. Most of the chairs seemed to be unclear about when they moved from one role to another. In order to be fair to the conferences, they needed to declare which hat they were wearing, so that the conference could be clear, but this was not referred to in the interviews and it had to be deduced that the chairs were not aware of the way they changed hats or, if they were aware, they did not declare it in the interviews or the conferences. Either way, their attempts at being objective and neutral assumed a different perspective.

12 The child and the parents

The literature search had suggested that there were many theoretical models available to use when chairing meetings. If the chairs were conjuring with all or some of them, as well as the practical aspects of, for example, late-comers or smokers in a non-smoking room, how did they managed to keep the child in mind? Was there a way in which they could relate to what was happening to the individual child, whilst in the middle of a formal procedure? The question asked was, 'How do you keep the individual child in mind?'

Brenda and Pete found no difficulty,

> It's not a problem now because I've been doing it three years and I'm more confident and competent. We keep the objective of the conference in mind and keep an open mind about it.
>
> No not difficult to keep the child in mind.

Bill, however, saw the problem from a different angle. He had already referred previously to an anxiety about standards. How was it possible to maintain standards of consistency in decision-making whilst conferencing so many children?

> It's very individualistic in a case conference but if I came back to pull out the last dozen case conferences I chaired, the worry I have is whether I have been consistent. Some children would have been registered in one conference and the same set of factors in another conference, they would not have been registered. I try and come back to the criteria for registration each time and discuss with colleagues but you get a bit blase about doing conferences as such.

Ivan acknowledged that in Review conferences he found difficulty in being clear which child it was.

... no problem with an initial case conference because of the way they're structured and it's the first time I've heard of the family. In review conferences there have been times when similar incidents creep into my mind, which is why I read the minutes shortly before.

Abe and Maude were particular about reminding themselves of the purpose of the conference,

> I like to look at the child in a holistic way when I go into a conference. I remind myself and the conference that we're here for child protection and other issues are secondary.

> I'm very conscious of that child and I always read the file beforehand and I try and be very clear about what we're talking about.

Others found difficulties:

> You have to try.

> It is a problem to think of the individual child because I've never met or seen the child. Until I do the impact doesn't hit me. I do have to put a lot of effort into this.

> One of the difficulties is sorting out the time-scale re the different children. Some children come over more clearly than others. If I'd met these children (the subjects of the context conference) I wouldn't have known them.

Ernest placed the question in a larger social work context. He had no comment about his own part in actively centring on the child.

> This is a mega question which is to do with social work – from little acorns ... and is about giving credibility and respect to anyone who makes contact.

Jim's simple analogy of etching a picture of the child, provided the clearest illustration of how possible it was to personalise what might easily become just another bureaucratic procedure.

> I start etching a picture of this child – how he fits with his family – his parents and if there are sibs – and I try and have a sketch of him in that family circle – and then at school and so on.

This provides a nice formula for a difficult process. It seems to allow for development and creativity about the child as well as drawing on factual information brought to the conference. But the answers to the question suggest some blurring about the individual child. Given that both Blom-Cooper (1987) and Butler-Sloss (1988) emphasise the crucial importance of focusing on the child in the conference, these answers show how difficult a task it is. Achieving a child focus in practice is not as easy as it sounds. There was recognition of the complexity of family dynamics, because the chairs were social workers and accustomed to complicated family situations but they appeared to struggle and seemed on the whole, to find the problem insoluble. Would it be possible for a child protection conference to be focused on the child at the same time as being focused on the business?

Part of the answer may lie in considering the presence of parents in conferences. It may be possible to link their presence with keeping the focus on the child if the chairing of the conference is clear.

Parental involvement in child protection conferences was already prescribed in Working Together (1988) but is more strongly advocated in Working Together (1991). There are a number of small scale studies produced during the early 1990s by individual local authorities evaluating their own pilot schemes (Hackney, Gloucestershire, Lewisham, Essex, Cumbria, Wiltshire, Bradford, Calderdale, N. Yorkshire, Berkshire), all of which favour parents being present. The trend is towards greater participation by parents and a recognition of the importance of preparing them to be participants and not just observers. There are implications for chairing when such policies are introduced and so a question about the chairs' reactions to the presence of parents in the conferences was necessary in the current climate. They had all seriously considered the issue and none was against it in principle. Their responses ranged from the pro-active to the protective. Three of the chairs had parents in all the way through the conference; two for most of the conference; one for a small part and eight not at all or only after the conference had finished.

Bill, Pete and Abe were all enthusiastic and in favour:

> I'd like more and more for parents to be at the case conference to hear (what is being said).

> One of the great advantages was that the parents could hear what everyone was saying. When parents are there the chair is called upon to be a skilful communicator more than anything else.

> Sometimes the parents make the better decisions.

George had chaired conferences with parents in for five years or more and 'wouldn't go back.'

Nancy and Greg were pragmatic:

> I am convinced they (parents) can deal with it but professionals can't. If you're rational and straight, they take it on board. I say 'We've had a discussion and this is the view of the conference. If you object you have a right to take it elsewhere.' I ask them if they would like to make a comment, how they would like to make it.

> I've always thought parents should be involved but the great difficulty is that if everyone isn't happy, what sort of conference do you end up with? I'd like parents to hear it all, otherwise we waste time and energy (i.e. re-running the conference to them).

Four of the chairpersons thought it problematical:

> Yes, in principle, but it's directly related to the varying degrees of quality of our social work staff and that is reflected in their relations with their clients. I'm acutely aware that some social workers wouldn't prepare parents for conferences and this would create situations that would be in no-one's interest.

> I'm aware that they (parents) change the nature of the conference.

> Bringing parents in creates hidden agendas in other agencies because they have different expectations. I'm committed to it ... basic human rights but there are an awful lot of skills needed.

> I think it's really vital ... it's the tone of the whole of Working Together but I still have real difficulties about Sexual Abuse ones. Parents do feel left out.

The remaining five chairpersons were paternal and protective about parents being present,

> The plan might include therapy for the parents and that would be difficult for them.

> I was sweating on the top line at the thought of having parents in and I spent a lot of time talking to them prior to the conference. In the conference the language was slightly different. Everything was said more carefully.

> You have to be careful about the language. Sometimes it's a horrible decision. It's a fairer way of doing things but it's not easy for them.

> Facing parents with all these people is awful for them – asking them to say all those awful things in front of all those people, and so I try to accommodate them to enable them to talk. I feel quite responsible for that ...

If the empathic social work skill of standing in the other's shoes leads to a paternalistic and protective view of handling parents then the result does not fit well with the view that parents are adults and capable of making responsible decisions for themselves and their children. Paternalism may lead to an infantilisation of parents and may create a dependency where the parent cannot act in a mature way regarding their children. Preparation of parents for the conference is essential and all the chairs were aware of this. The brisk pragmatic approach which assumed that parents would be present and would therefore need to know the procedures as a foundation to their participation fitted better with the ideas of personhood and citizen's rights so often quoted in this debate which is more likely to lead to partnership. The chairs were also aware of their own need to develop their communication skills. Ben summed the dilemmas up succinctly:

At court parents have their own representatives and have an equal status – are parties to the proceedings and don't need to be looked after in quite the same way ... We need to be serious about the representation of parents in order to be serious about participation. We have to be much more serious about every component of the case conference. But if chairs and staff are well-prepared they might be well ahead of the parents – being there in the body isn't enough. Inducting people into the meeting is important, showing by example, being congruent.

Many of the responses suggested an anxiety about the presence of parents and whether the chairs would have the ability to chair, given the potential difficulties surrounding their presence. The anxieties appeared to rest in three areas. Firstly, whether the parents could cope. Secondly whether social workers and other agencies could cope and thirdly whether they as chairs could cope. All of these anxieties could be addressed rather simply by training for everyone and such a solution seems obvious. Why then do the chairs remain anxious? Most of them imply uncertainty because of the unknown. At periods of change people tend to resist before they enter the process of uncertainty prior to the actual change. Conferences had been in the past, fairly safe arenas for the discussion of client families, even though they might sometimes cause dissension between professionals. The presence of parents would be an unknown and therefore unsafe arena for at least eight of the chairs. Three more of the chairs had experience of parents being in for only part of the conference which has been found since (Marchant and Luckham 1992 and Thoburn 1992) to be a more difficult arrangement at least for parents. The remaining three chairs would know of the real uncertainties of chairing whilst parents were present throughout, but even they still confessed to some anxiety.

Musicians and actors in the performing arts almost always confess to some stress and anxiety before performance and accept that the adrenalin it produces tends to give an edge to their performance which would be missing if their affect was flat. Whilst chairing child protection conferences is one task in a repertoire of many for the chairs, it also contains this aspect of public performance and therefore is likely to carry with it the same stress and anxiety. The respondents in this study seemed to refer to anxieties and difficulties beyond the performance stress. They focused on how to keep the child in mind and how to accommodate parents in the conferences appropriately.

Training and experience are methods of ensuring confidence in chairing but as we have seen, none of the chairs in this study had received the kind of training which encompassed the complexities of chairing child protection conferences, nor had the majority, as yet, had the experience of chairing with parents present. Seeing and hearing the child in the flesh in a conference is a certain way of keeping her/him in mind. Seeing and hearing parents in a conference also brings the child more clearly to mind because of the information brought by the parents, which only they possess. The chairing skills required to enable children and parents to participate in conferences are wider though not necessarily different from those required to chair a meeting of professionals. What has to be addressed is the issue of the power differential between the family and the professionals. The chairperson using the business method in the conference may achieve some balance of power by sharing the information with family members beforehand and by preparing them for the conference and involving them as the conference proceeds. Holding the child in the forefront of their mind as the principal reason for holding the conference but in practice using the business method for gaining information about the child, aiming for jargon-free language and acknowledging the particular difficulties which parents will have in such a meeting, but without letting them dominate, should ensure that the chairs keep the individual child real and alive for the conference members.

13 The chairs' attitudes to child abuse and neglect

The national congress of the British Association for the Study and Prevention of Child Abuse and Neglect (BASPCAN) in Leicester September 1991, focused on the importance of conveying research to the public as well as to professionals. The congress was told that professional workers, in the past, discovered the symptoms of abuse and neglect and had to generate their own theory about it. They shared information about incidence and prevalence amongst themselves, found helping responses, invented treatments and attempted evaluation whilst, at the same time, trying to convince a reluctant public of the extent and severity of child abuse and neglect without causing alarm and despondency.

Margaret Lynch, Rupert Hughes and Helen Agathanos spoke of the importance of keeping in touch with the public, seeking public support for the frameworks of operation in child protection procedures and of taking account of the cross-cultural dimensions of child abuse. Unless professional workers involved in child protection work have definitions and explanations to offer the public which are differentiated from individual value systems and gut feelings, it is likely that public opinion will continue to oscillate between ongoing ignorance and flat panic at times of crisis. Social workers are only too well aware that the media are more likely to whip up attitudes of self-righteous indignation and blame, rather than understanding or informed tolerance.

Did the chairs see themselves as pivotal in any way in relation to attitudes to child abuse in the wider context? Were they familiar with research findings in child abuse and how to use them in their task of chairing, or did they rely solely on practice wisdom, much as social work as a profession has done in the past?

A question to seven of the chairs about their own attitudes to abuse and neglect produced responses about disadvantaged families being highly represented in child protection procedures and a wish to acknowledge it by greater tolerance.

> It's a combination of things where children have been victimised as a result of poverty and what-have-you ... lack of resources and also a pathology in terms of parents not having had the benefit of caring relationships.

> I have strong feelings about the people who come to us because most of the cases are people on low incomes, working class, and single mothers. My tolerance level is higher for them. We have to make allowances for the economic and social pressures they cope with. Upper social classes hide behind boarding schools.

They also responded with more personal views:

> I have a high tolerance of what abuse or bad parenting or rough play is about, so I don't have a cosy middle-class view about middle-class parenting ... what is good enough.

> I don't have sympathy for the power theories of abuse. I've taken a special interest in aggression. It is a fundamental component of the human personality so I don't see violence in the evil way it's often presented. I don't see male abusers as intrinsically evil but more as damaged, locked into destructive patterns ... including sexual abuse.

> Some kinds of abuse affect me more than others ... a child describing how her father tied her with a dog lead to the stairs. I find it hard to cope with intentional abuse. I need to contemplate that. Doing social work you think you've heard it all and you wonder how human nature can be like that. I can be just as punitive and want to emasculate someone ...

> What I personally feel about abuse is that if the human condition is common to all of us, then we're all capable of it. To take up stances either anti to perpetrators or those who should protect isn't purposeful for the children. You're looking for crusades then. It's ever so simple to want to punish the abuser, blame the non-abusing parent and pass on a message to the children that what they feel about this person is not love and affection but something to be ashamed of and is awful.

Some of the chairs referred to the 'regular group' of attenders at their conferences and how over the years their joint understanding of abuse had grown:

> You do share understandings about what is happening. You do form a mode of thinking. There is still an immense range of views about abuse, particularly sexual abuse, but much less retribution upfront – that has changed over a period of time.

As far as we are concerned we have a philosophy of self-determination (for client families) and with regard to the travelling families if those are their standards about bringing up their children – and one doesn't thrive as well as the others, those are the things we try to work with. I think we have to aim for some kind of standard but embodied in all of that there has to be a strong element of sensitivity, of caring, of being skilled and knowledgeable enough to know when to push hard in a given situation.

I remember talking to parents about what we would expect a child of that age to have in her room in terms of warmth and possessions ... and the protection plan spelled out what we expected.

I hope to open people's minds up to wider things ... I might weave in some information/knowledge about child abuse ... point out some predisposing factors (so they) see it in the context of the whole ... holistic.

It is about abuse, poverty, chaotic families and personal standards all mixed in. We had case discussions and now they're case conferences and there's a development of a professional discussion. I can want to emasculate someone but the other part of me says, 'How can we educate people?' We ought to say 'It's wrong' ... child sexual abuse ... spell it out ... 'It's wrong' and if they break those rules ...

But some chairs repudiated the idea strongly:

I think that's arrogant.

I wouldn't do that (give information on abuse). I base it on what is before me in the conference. If you haven't got the evidence, you haven't got the evidence.

No I try to keep to the quality and pertinence of the information.

The best I can do is pick up what has been said ... a lot is third party, anecdotal and I try to put the facts first.

These replies express the non-judgemental social work view of families based on experience and practice wisdom. Other chairs found the question irrelevant. They regarded the primary and only purpose of the conference to be a decision-making meeting based on gathering evidence and having no connection with the wider world and therefore not requiring any consideration of research findings.

The notion that conferences might be, or should be, related to the public domain through the way families were viewed or through the way professionals defined child abuse and neglect in the conferences, was not one that the chairs were particularly attracted to, nor saw as part of a chairing function. Some thought that the conferences might include and disseminate information from research findings but the general view of the nature of the conference was that it was about gathering information. Whilst expressing tolerant views about the families, they did not relate this to a wider context of abuse and neglect.

Parents regard conferences as quasi-judicial settings in any case, where the professionals have already made up their minds about the incident of abuse or neglect (Thoburn 1992) and where the power imbalance does not favour families. The combination for a chairperson, of being responsible for running a meeting which expresses fairness to parents and child, whether they are present or not, and ensuring that the risk of abuse or neglect is adequately addressed, presents a major challenge to their skills. It requires stringency and sharpness about the information presented whilst maintaining warmth and empathy. In order to maintain warmth and empathy the chairperson needs a wider understanding of what is before her/him in the conference and therefore a ready access to both research findings and public opinion to generate balance. Where these two aspects of unbiased information and professional attributes cross, independence and neutrality are likely to have a better chance of working. There is also a case to be made, as Corby has done (1993) for improving and informing practice through the use of research findings especially in the field of child abuse because of the importance of developing a body of theory for the social work profession to draw on as well as practice wisdom.

14 Is there a 'better' case conference?

Professionals refer to some conferences being 'better' than others. Did the people who chaired the conferences hold this view too and to what might they attribute it? The question was 'Do you think there are "better" conferences than others and why?' One idea was that they might take the responsibility for the quality of the conference upon themselves as the chair. In fact, only Bill did. He said that in his opinion the most consistent reason for the variation in the conferences was the chairperson. All the others said it depended on who else was present, and whether they contributed and the quality of their contributions. Maude put it most clearly:

> A better case conference is one where everyone present has had a chance to say what is necessary and important to say; where they've been heard; where everyone is clear about what was said and decided. You can only go round and check. I can't read people's minds. I can only hope that the balance of the conference between formality and ease is right.

She graphically described one which was not like that!

> It ended up like a WI tea-party. I expected them to be talking about jam-making next.

The respondents appeared to regard the process of the conference as the source of what might be 'better' but they did not relate better process to better outcome. The literature on decision-making and leadership skills strongly suggests that the two are inter-related. A leader or chairperson in a small group or conference needs to bear in mind two aspects which need furthering for the group to function well: task and maintenance. S/he needs to use a decision-making tree in order to gain information or evidence; to weigh it up; to seek more information or evidence preferably of an opposite nature; to weigh it up again; to seek expert advice; to summarise and to provide alternatives. The use of an active, open and honest style of chairing which allows for small decisions to lead into larger decisions provides for an optimal environment for decision-making. The whole process tends to be co-operative and not authoritarian. Some of the chairs had some of these dimensions clearly in their minds and appeared to be using them usefully but no respondent seemed to have a clear grasp of all the dimensions of chairing which were accessible to them and which if used, would improve their skills in relation to child protection conferences.

A second question asked whether if the 'better' case conferences lay beyond their control, did the chairpersons think that they were being asked to carry out a function in the child protection procedures which was not appropriate? Did they have to try and make an outmoded piece of machinery work? None of them went so far as to dismiss the conferences but none was uncritical of them.

> Yes, they are still important if they are not over-used and if they are managed well. They can be a very good vehicle for engaging people ... a tool ... a part of the process.

> They've got to be used properly.

> Yes, I'd keep them but sometimes there isn't the level of discussion and debate that there should be and that worries me. I don't know what it is. Sometimes they are dry ... it's just hard work.

> They don't promote the discussion they should and they haven't achieved their aims. It depends on whether the ACPCs (Area Child Protection Committees) work. Ours have planning meetings ... a cluster of meetings which make the conferences blurred round the edges. It's quite confusing. The most important part of the conference is the gate-keeping.

> The case conference seems to me rather like a machine that sets into action some functions that make you think 'Are there better ways of doing this?' It becomes too formalised. Are there any more profound things decided at a case conference than would have been done anyway?

> It's terribly ritualised and sometimes destroys the creative approach. It's sometimes better to have a crisis and get something out in the open. You can throw buckets of water on beforehand but not solve anything.

Three chairs were more positive and thought that despite its deficiencies the case conference was still crucial.

> I still think it's very important for all professionals in a case to meet together and agree a plan of work. Whether I'd call it a case conference is debatable ... but that type of meeting is still required.

> The case conference is the best place so far for making judgements about the protection of the child but it's not the best place to have the conversations about the distress caused to professionals and public.

I couldn't conceive of treating this particular work without the case conference. The case conference is the embodiment of all of our work. I view the case conference as the single most important thing (in the child protection procedures). It's more than an exchange of information. It aids clearer thinking and decision-making and planning.

This discussion reflected the dilemma for the people who chaired conferences in fulfilling their role adequately. On the one hand, whilst acknowledging their personal role and the importance of their own skill in chairing the conferences, what emerged more clearly on the other, was the weight of factors affecting the quality of the conferences which they thought were beyond their influence. These ranged from a recognition of the necessity to have a meeting of everyone concerned and sharing information and planning for the protection of the child, to the unseen weight of gate-keeping the conferences and how to gain quality information for the conference. One chairperson illustrated it by making the point that individuals may be as expert and skilful as the best, but if the structures behind the conferences, responsible for standards of work and commitment to the procedures, are not congruent, then the chairperson cannot produce these qualities on his or her own.

This section indicates more clearly than some of the others that most of the chairs saw the act of chairing as dependent on the procedures and on the other members of the conference being accountable for the quality of their contributions and not on the level of their own standards of chairing and what that might comprise in terms of quality of information given, preparation, expert advice and open-ness about the process and their role in it. It seemed that they regarded the success or failure of the conference as being beyond their immediate control.

Part III

Part III

15 An overview of chairing child protection conferences

> *We should ask ourselves what in our child protection procedures we do to protect and strengthen the relationships between parents and children to enable parents to fulfil their parental responsibilities, or whether there is anything in those procedures that undermines that position. If we do not arrive at an empowering process for our conferences we will reduce the chance of parents contributing to the plans we make.* (David Monk, quoted in Thoburn, 1992)

In order to achieve a view of the conferences which was one step removed from the mechanics of chairing and to seek a more holistic idea of what was going on in the conferences, time was spent listening to the tapes on a different level. It was not so much, this time, to what the chairs were saying but to the way in which they said it. There were nuances of tone in the replies, inflections of voice, many sighs, some laughter and jokes, pauses, asides and a range of expressed emotion which was reflected upon in relation to the content of the tapes. The prevailing descriptions were of the complexities of the task. The chairs did not convey a picture of an ordinary everyday sort of meeting. They strove to make sense of a preponderance of experienced difficulties in conducting the conferences. Two questions at the end of the interviews led to a view of the whole task of chairing and why the chairs may have found the task so difficult. The answers to these two questions gave rise to further ideas about what may have caused the heavy emphasis in the tapes to be on the problems connected with chairing.

One of the requests was for an analogy which the chairs would use to describe a case conference. It was rather a sting in the tail and evoked some very long silences and one horrified reply, 'I'm completely stunned by that ... !' but the answers reinforced the view of a meeting difficult to manage.

Five of the analogies were of things which were difficult to handle:

> an octopus
>
> trying to hold water in your hands
>
> an unwieldy mechanism
>
> a big ferret
>
> should be an owl but feels like a bull terrier – or at times a rottweiler!

Seven replies likened the conference to a traditional or formal meeting of some kind:

> a kangaroo court with a touch of the Old Vic – something stage-managed
>
> a forum
>
> it's a court-room
>
> a business executive meeting
>
> like being magistrates or a judge
>
> more a judicial meeting
>
> an old boys' club – ossified!

The final two were in a constructive, creative vein, though one clearly implied labour:

> lego
>
> giving birth instead of remaining pregnant

What the chairs found themselves engaged in was a professional social occasion, the true nature of which was unpredictable. The guidelines had given them a list of things they had to deal with but not a format for dealing with them. The child protection conferences were not governed by clear rules or conventions, nor were they common or garden meetings able to function solely under business agendas. Each chairperson was left to work out for her/himself, as best they could, how to go about chairing them.

The other question was, 'What would you say you bring to chairing from your own belief system?' The replies varied:

> I feel that the bottom line is, parents have to provide for their children, so I regard my understanding of parenting important.
>
> trying to be honest
>
> it's about justice
>
> common sense and my own experience

Other phrases were: 'right to be heard,' 'intellectual honesty,' 'it's a serious business and you must behave yourselves,' 'doing it properly.' There emerged a clear sense from the replies that the chairs wished to be fair in what they did, both towards parents and to children. Nine of the chairs used words or phrases which indicated their commitment to being fair or who used the word 'justice.' Three specifically referred to the rights of the child or what was best for the child and the remaining two responses were about an optimistic belief in people and using common sense. This sense of fairness might spring from empathising with parents' positions of powerlessness and injustice because experience tells the chairs that the conference itself is unpredictable and therefore an unfair model for arriving at decisions. Conscious of their social work roots, the chairs might have a heightened awareness of the need to be fair in a personal way, although the structure of most of the conferences made this virtually impossible. Those who emphasised the 'rights of the child' might believe they were responsible for reaching the 'right' decision for the child and would do so on behalf of the conference or ensure that the conference reached a 'right' decision for the child. In either case, there appeared to be a mismatch between the unpredictability of the conference and the model of fairness and rights which chairs endeavoured to put into practice.

Not only were the chairs without clear conventions and rules as to the conduct of the conferences but also without clear guidance regarding the decision-making about registration. The chairs knew that the decision to register was the only decision of the conference but they were unclear as to whether it was to be a collective decision or their own decision. To whom were they accountable for this decision? How were they to 'do a good job' and 'do it properly' if they did not know whether 'properly' was a conference decision or their own personal decision?

It was possible to analyse this mismatch further by drawing out from the tapes, the aims the chairs had for the conferences, their self-reported actions in the conferences and comparing the two.

What the chairs aimed for

In order to clarify what the conferences were like, phrases in the tapes like: 'I try ...'; 'I like to ...'; 'I want ...', were sought as indicators of what the chairs were aiming for. Then in a more general way what they said they did was extracted in order to set the two findings alongside each other. In this way it would be possible to discover whether they did what they said they aimed at. Their comments about what they aimed for were reminiscent of the preparations which might be made for guests coming to a meal: creating an ambience of ease, planning timing, setting the table and finding the drinks beforehand so that the evening would run smoothly; and using resources – recipes and ingredients from the larder, and galvanising cooking skills to achieve it.

Similarly, the chairs spoke of:

1) Generating an atmosphere 'not too formal, not too easy'; 'setting the climate'; and of using their social work skills to do this: 'I try to get people to listen so they see the whole context'; 'I try very hard for it not to be social services conference'; 'I like to be collaborative'; 'I want to be enabling ...'; 'I try and be tactful'. These were aims about handling people kindly and sympathetically in a social work tradition. The chairs spoke quietly on the tapes but with positive feelings. They wanted to create an ambience in which the meeting could take place without stress.

2) Aiming at running the meeting smoothly by using some foresight: 'I try to get there early to meet people coming in'; 'I try to get everyone to contribute'; 'stop other agendas'; 'I'd look at some realistic options'; 'I try not to be totally blind beforehand. Obviously you fish around a little bit so you know what you're doing'; 'I try and be clear about the issues to start with'; 'I want to ensure the whole is heard and the conclusion a consensus.' These describe practical action and mental action, indicating what it is the chairs intend should happen in their conferences. They were said assertively and firmly and were about the structure of the conferences.

3) Making sure the meeting runs well, as a process. This involved their own role as the chairperson and illustrated what they wanted to do. 'I try and whittle down the information so we can deal with it'; 'I pull everything together to try and make sense of it'; 'I like to be ordered'; 'I try and gather what is the truest story of all'; 'I try and keep it on track'; 'I try and focus on the facts'; 'I try and set the standards about the quality of the information.' These were how they attempted to shape the content of the conferences by using strategies. These are their own chairing resources. These phrases were said with what appeared to be a degree of hope.

The aims of the chairs were congruent with ways of running meetings competently but there was a preponderance of references in the tapes to their struggles to achieve these aims. The deduction has to be made, that the difficulties in achieving them were always present in the task.

Somehow, the experience of chairing many conferences had not resolved the problems. It was as though there was an acceptance that conferences were difficult, awkward exercises. There was no reference to the possibility of learning how to do it better to make it less difficult.

What the chairs said they did

The descriptions of what the chairs said they did focused heavily on the need to gain and discuss the information or evidence. They referred to it in a more urgent way than to other parts of the interview. The emphasis in the tapes in terms of the time spent describing the conferences, was on this aspect. It seemed to provoke the most anxiety because the chairs believed that the rest of the conference depended upon how well it was achieved. They connected the decision about registration to the quality of this part of the conference. Only surprisingly few tapes had an emphasis on the protection plan which follows the decision about registration. Whereas all three parts of the conferences are inter-related, the weight of the conference as described by the chairs was towards the link between evidence and registration.

Working Together (1991) clearly defines the purpose of the conference as 'not a forum for a formal decision that a person has abused a child' but for 'sharing information and concerns, analysis of risk and recommending responsibility for action,' (6.1) but the chairs who were interviewed were working from Working Together (1988) which has a slightly different emphasis from the 1991 version about the purpose of conferences. It speaks of a 'multi-disciplinary discussion of allegations or suspicions of abuse; the outcome of investigation; assessments for planning; an action plan for protecting the child and helping the family and reviews of the plan' (5.39). So although there are similarities in the versions, if account is taken of the different philosophy of partnership underlying the 1991 version, there is a shift in 1991 towards considering the future risk of harm to the child and what needs to be planned, rather than the main focus in 1988 on what had happened in the past and judging whether abuse or neglect had taken place.

The tapes revealed an emphasis on gaining evidence for the abuse or neglect for the purpose of registration and not on the protection plan or action to follow. It could be argued that if there was no registration, then there was no need for a protection plan so the first step was to establish whether the allegation was true and the child at risk. It could also be argued from the comments in the tapes, that the protection plan did not cause the chairs as much difficulty as gaining the information and discussing it. The descriptions about the protection plans were in terms of the multi-disciplinary aspect of the conference and the usefulness of working together. They were positive and optimistic in tone and they did not appear to present the same problems to the chairs as the information-gathering stage. There are a number of other possible reasons why the chairs focused on the first part of the conference. One in particular attracted consideration.

A number of comments prompted the idea of which the following are examples:

> It's the best place for making judgements about what is going on – what evidence is corroborated.

> Case conferences can be split about whether they believe the parent or not.

> It's like hearing evidence in court. You can't be emotional about it. You have to cut it (emotion) off.

There's much less retribution up front now. At one time it felt like 'let's get the bastards.' It was a helluva place to be, especially if you were a male.

A pseudo-court

Most of the respondents used the language of judgement about this stage of the conference. They appeared to have become caught into the model of the conference as a pseudo-court and not the model of a joint multi-agency/family exercise in sharing information and concerns and actions. There are a number of possibilities why this might have been so. It might relate to a wider view, prevalent among many professionals, about child abuse and neglect which uses a disease model (Parton 1985, Stevenson 1989) or a dangerous families model (Dale et al 1986) which leads to looking for 'signs' or ticking checklists of risk factors. It might relate to the difficulties the chairs spoke of in getting the non-social work professionals to present facts and not hearsay. Hearsay tends to enlarge suspicion and may influence a conference unduly (Moore 1985). There are subtle differences between 'information' and 'evidence' and between 'suspicion' and 'concern' and therefore it might relate to a semantic question. Nevertheless it raises the issue of balance in the conference between collecting information to illuminate what has happened and seeking evidence to allocate responsibility or lay blame for the abuse or neglect which has occurred and the role of the chairperson in achieving that balance. Professional workers may have already made up their minds `at street level' about the family and the chairs may have to try and make sense of a wide diversity of personal views. Professional assessment may be lacking and have to be sought. One chairperson was aware of the dilemma:

> Chairs are not trained to weigh evidence – only High Court judges are trained to do that so the best I can do is pick up what has been said. The case conference needs to paint a picture ...

Whereas in the past, case conferences started out as a benevolent, paternalistic medical model with professionals trying to help families in a nurturing mode and formulating treatment plans for them, the conferences, at the time of the interviews, were struggling with being objective meetings but subject to gossip, hidden agendas, and unsubstantiated opinion, about which all the respondents complained. Their conferences were neither the new model advocated in Working Together (1991) in which it is intended that professionals and families should participate together in the same endeavour of protecting the child, nor yet the old paternalistic model. They appeared to be struggling with a judgement model and they seemed to have fallen into the trap of trying evidence about families, like a court, without being set up to do so. They were therefore giving themselves the invidious job of achieving litigious decisions by agreement. In putting themselves in the position of being judge of the information or trying to make the conference judge it, they had added an aspect to the task of chairing which they could not carry out in a way which they thought would be fair to families and congruent with social work ethics. They found themselves in an uncomfortable seat. They said that keeping control of the discussion about the evidence and getting the conference to own decisions was hard work, especially when the evidence for that decision might be poorly presented and biased. When the decision was united, the chairs were satisfied. They spoke with relief about the very few occasions that any of them had experienced, when they had been obliged to record a minority view but they spoke with furrowed brows about the difficulties of 'getting them to form conclusions,' as though even this was not to their satisfaction. *Judging* is to try and decide questions of law and guiltiness, or to compare facts to determine the truth. *Deciding* is to settle or resolve something, or to make up one's mind. The difference is subtle yet in the context of child protection, has consequences beyond two neutral definitions.

It appeared from the tapes that focusing on judging evidence about what had happened for the purposes of registration, slanted the conference towards concentrating on how the abuse or neglect had occurred and who was responsible and not towards evaluating the risk of harm to the child in the future and the balance of the strengths and difficulties of the families in the context of protection. In trying to weigh up who was responsible and whether the details of the abuse or neglect were consistent with the explanations, the conference leaned towards difficulties which could not always be resolved, rather than balancing positive and negative information. As has been illustrated in the literature on the difficulty of identifying traits of abusive families, such traits may be found in all families if they are sought. 'It will be clear that many families in which abuse occurs are families which have for a long time been in need of help. It is therefore important ... to formulate one's goals not in the negative terms implied by the concept of "prevention" but in a detailed positive programme which aims to improve the family's whole pattern of interaction and quality of life.' (Lynch and Roberts 1977) The chairs did not refer to the need for positive aspects and strengths of families to be considered in conjunction with negative information and for both to be evaluated in relation to the issue of the protection of the child. Parents who have attended child protection conferences report a focus on negative information about themselves. They equate the experience of attending conferences to that of a court where the professionals' minds have already been made up before they arrived (Thoburn and Shemmings 1990; Shemmings 1991; Burns 1991; Luckham and Marchant 1992). Assessing risk only on negative information is bound to produce evidence of risk. However, it may be the case that there is only negative information about some of the families. Should this be so it would be unusual and the chairperson would be alerted to the gravity of the implications. Nevertheless for 60 per cent or more of the families who come within the child protection procedures there is no decision to remove the child from home. (Children and Young Persons on Child Protection Registers 1991)

Working Together (1988) says, 'The entry of the child's name on the register should normally only occur following discussion at a case conference when abuse or potential abuse is confirmed and an inter-agency agreement is made to work co-operatively.' (5.32)

In Working Together (1991) the decision to register must also be made at a child protection conference and 'the conference must decide that there is, or is a likelihood of, significant harm leading to the need for a child protection plan. One of the following requirements needs to be satisfied:

i) There must be one or more identifiable incidents which can be described as having adversely affected the child. They may be acts of commission or omission. They can be either physical, sexual, emotional or neglectful. It is important to identify a specific occasion or occasions when the incident has occurred. Professional judgement is that further incidents are likely;

or

ii) Significant harm is expected on the basis of professional judgement of the findings of the investigation in this particular case or on research evidence'.

Note that the next sentence *follows* the requirement for the conference to decide that a protection plan is needed.

> The conference will need to establish so far as they can a cause of the harm or likelihood of harm. (Para. 6.39)

In the 1991 list of purposes for the conference registration is only one part of the process and appears halfway through: 'to share and evaluate the information gathered during investigation, to make decisions about the level of risk to the child(ren), to decide on the need for registration and to make plans for the future.' (6.5) The use of the words 'decide on the need for registration' and not just on entering the child's name on the register, adds a slightly different connotation from that drawn from the references to registration in the tapes. It appeared that the people who chaired the conferences had tended to become focused on seeking a 'true' version of the abuse and were linking it to registration rather than the need for a protection plan, This was very much in line with the emphasis in Working Together (1988) but it appeared to be to the detriment of the family and other aims of the conference because it led to judicial behaviour. As a result the chairs had added to the complexities of their chairing role. The focus on registration in the context of abuse and neglect had inevitably led them to make judgements about parents, often without parents being there and on information which often did not include parents' or the child's views. A major part of the families' information was missing from the picture. The chairs were in a leadership position responsible for asking for evidence about the abuse or neglect, selecting it, and making or gaining a judgement about its veracity on negative and inadequate content, instead of making a decision about the need for a child to be protected based on the positive and negative information about the family as well as the abuse and neglect.

The judgement model and parental participation

The introduction of the principle of parental participation in conferences should help to move the focus from judging evidence, to safeguarding the child. The presence of parents and the importance of working in partnership with parents under the Children Act, makes the conference a different kind of meeting (Thoburn et al 1992).

There were five people who chaired conferences where parents already attended, if not for all the conference, at least for the major part of it. Were these conferences conducted any differently? In one such observed conference the parents were invited but did not attend and although they were not present, the chairperson thought they were coming and was prepared for them to be present. The decision to register the child in the category of non-organic Failure to Thrive was hotly contested by some of the professionals present even though the consultant paediatrician, who was also present, had made that diagnosis and thought registration necessary. The chairperson confessed to me afterwards that he had no option but to accept the strength of feeling in the conference against registration despite the fact that the answer to the question, 'Was this child failing to thrive?' was 'Yes'. The reason for opposing registration by three professionals who were in the frontline with the family was that the parents, particularly the mother, would be so upset and undermined by registration that it would be impossible to engage her in the work. (The same diagnosis had been made on her first child and successful work had been undertaken at the Family Centre.) In the conference the chairperson had listened to and accepted the diagnosis of likely harm if the current situation continued but then had listened to the weight of the views of the professionals involved who knew that in the past the family had succeeded in enabling the first child to thrive by using the resources provided. He had taken, as well, their representation of the wishes of the parents in the matter towards working together on a protection plan. He demonstrated a willingness to move off the past abuse/neglect focus onto a focus for the future work with the family which would protect the child. So although technically it could be argued that the child should have been registered, in this case the chairperson had shifted the focus from abuse to protection and been influenced by the workers' views of the positive use made of the previous voluntary arrangement. If this could happen without the parents being physically present, although they were expected, then it seems likely that had they been present to state their own case, this more balanced view would have been even more likely to prevail.

The question of maintaining balance in the conference relates to the decision-making literature, in that competent decision-making rests not only on seeking all the information, but also evaluating it in the light of opposite information. None of the chairs described doing this as part of their chairing skills, so that in focusing on gaining evidence about the incident and who was responsible for the abuse or neglect they set up a negative view of the family in the conference. The chairs who had parents attending were able to check accuracy and facts with them and ensure that their views would be heard, enabling other information to be introduced and for all of it to be evaluated in relation to the whole. The use of the requirements for registration in Working Together (1991), before considering the categories of abuse encourages the focus on the future.

Other aspects of what the chairs said they did

Although the main descriptions of what the chairs said they did, were about gaining information or evidence at the start of the conference, they also described other actions. For example, some mentioned making sure that the key professionals were invited to the conference and that invitations were sent to specialists if they were required to inform the conference with their expertise. Some would challenge poor contributions to the conferences afterwards. Some would try, during the conference, to keep the process 'on track' and bring members back to the point when necessary. The tapes were punctuated in these sections by sighs and pauses. Their tenor was serious and sometimes a little depressed as the respondents tried to get to grips with describing the difficulties of the task.

One other interesting theme in the tapes was what the chairs said they did in connection with conflict. It would be pushing their descriptions to suggest that they avoided conflict or even that they tried to avoid it, but nevertheless there were a number of comments which implied this:

> I count out those who don't help (i.e. he does not allow conflictual contributions to influence).

> Once the shit hits the fan, professionals retreat into stereotypes. Conflict can be about attitude or handling. It's easier now, because we've worked together already. It (conflict)'s only helpful when we have an understanding of each other. We can recognise it and can deal with it. (doubtful tone)

> There are conferences that leave you thinking 'this is a can of worms with no bottom' and kicking yourself if it's not clear and you haven't done it well enough.

These are not comments which suggest the chairs sought out disagreement as part of their task. There were no comments about addressing disagreement or conflict by drawing attention to it and seeking ways from the members about how to resolve it. We may have assumed in child protection that if we intended fairness and endeavoured to provide a relaxed atmosphere in conferences, that conflict would not occur and that if it did, it was the failure of the chairs to 'get it right.' It would be more realistic, especially in a child protection conference, to expect disagreement and welcome it as necessary and to have skills at the ready to deal with it.

Comparing aims and actions

First aim and reported actions

Did the people who chaired conferences do what they said they aimed to do? If we balance the first part of the first aim, of creating an unstressed atmosphere to enable discussion to take place, with the reported stress for the chairs in managing that part of the conference, the answer appears to be 'No.' Their descriptions suggest that in any case, the nature of the meeting produces tension and disagreement. Members may be explicitly disagreeing or ominously not. Therefore aiming for an unstressed atmosphere was unrealistic and probably a waste of nervous energy. Tensions exist in conferences. To deal with the second part of the first aim, of handling people kindly, we must turn to the style of the chairs as described in chapter 11. A 'social work' style was maintained by most of the chairs throughout the meeting but a minority used a 'barrister' style to achieve their aims. Both styles enabled the conference to carry out its business. But practising social work skills in which the chairs were experienced and with which they would feel comfortable, to deal with the conference members, seems pragmatic and sensible. The 'barrister' chairs were the ones who spoke of the need to control the conference. Moore (1992) says, 'Chairs need to feel secure enough to tease out differences and to act occasionally as devil's advocate if the group has agreed too quickly without looking at all the alternatives' (p. 166). The repertoire of social work skills should come into its own here not necessarily to dominate the conference nor to provide a comfortable session but to purposefully gather the information and seek opposite information. The tapes suggest that the chairs did not make this distinction and were attempting to adopt a personal style of 'enabling' throughout the conference or of 'controlling' throughout the conference, neither of which was entirely satisfactory to them.

Second aim and reported actions

The second aim of being prepared, in the sense of having ideas or a mental map of the way the chairs wanted the conference to run, appeared to be successful in their terms. Their over-riding purpose was to make the decision about registration and they used the word 'consensually' or 'consensus' to describe their mental model. They reported that in only a few conferences did they have to record a minority view of disagreement. Using this as a measure to decide that the second aim was fulfilled, has problems because there is no way of knowing whether members were really satisfied with the whole conference and not just with the decision about registration. We only know they were not so disgruntled that they wanted to make a stand against the decision to register and after all, registration is a safe one for professionals. A number of the chairs spoke of the `belt and braces' approach to registration taken by many members of the conferences. The influence of `groupthink' which would operate against disagreement would be another factor to note. The aim of having a mental map for conferences could be helpful but tied to a particular way of making decisions could be powerfully influential. The chairs who did not make the decision about registration themselves hoped to make it consensually but as we have seen in chapter 5, consensual decision-making tends not to take account of all the information. Tied to an autocratic decision such a map could inhibit the full interplay of information which might be outside the holder's imagination. However, practical and mental preparation before a conference must not be criticised. It does contribute a plan or framework within which the conference may proceed. Most of the chairs put this aim into practice at least some of the time in their own way.

Third aim and reported actions

The third aim of how they wished to be active in the chairing role is difficult to assess because it is an evaluation, and without recorded observations of their conferences, cannot easily be measured. However, on their own descriptions of what they did, as they took the writer through a particular conference, it can be said they had made serious attempts at doing what they aimed for, even if, judging from their tones on the tapes, they found it frustrating and difficult. Some did count out members of the conference with no contact with the family in order to limit information. Some described 'chunking' the conference to make it more manageable and of summarising as it went along in order to make sense of all the information. Some rebuked members of the conference for making out-of-order remarks, during or after the conference. Some invited experts when needed, to set a context for the information and some would present alternative possible routes for members to go down to make decisions. All of these are the well-researched decision-making or leadership skills in the literature, but in contrast to the second category of aims, were not by any means attempted by all of the chairs. Yet it would be possible for them to do so. With adequate training in small group work, decision-making and leadership skills and with simple self-help schemes of asking a colleague to rate them on a list of such skills for later joint discussion, the chairs could easily improve their own skills.

Despite the rich data from the respondents about chairing, this study has not attempted detailed observations nor has it been able to systematically compare their aims and actions. Were this to be possible the chairing of child protection conferences could be more accurately charted and usefully evaluated for training purposes.

The difficulties in chairing

Meanwhile, we have discovered that the sources of the difficulties in the conferences are well-rehearsed as separate, complex subjects in the child protection literature.

- Child abuse and neglect in itself causes stress. Lynch (in Baglow 1990) bears this out when she says that the amount of pain workers feel 'deepens rather than lessens with time and experience.' Pottage and Evans (1992) describe the effects of stress on workers' behaviour leading to control and competition rather than co-operation and Menzies (1961) illustrates the tendency towards ritualistic behaviour as a defence mechanism when workers are faced with too much stress.
- Inter-professional behaviour, whilst providing wide cover for the protection of the child, also provides hidden agendas which can jeopardise the neutrality and objectivity of the chair if they try to defend social services staff and policies. Some professionals may never have attended a child protection conference and are unprepared emotionally and technically.
- 'Street level' assessments are made by workers in child protection; unsubstantiated statements are made in conferences and gossip may be perpetuated. There may be no discrimination between fact and opinion.
- Oppressive remarks about race, gender, age or disability may emerge in conferences because of a lack of sensitivity on the part of individual professionals. Equal Opportunities policies may exist but not operate unless the chairperson uses their role as chair to ensure they are followed.
- The decision about registration has no direct guidelines so technically the chairs in the study were free to make that particular decision themselves, as some of them did, or to gain a decision from the conference members, as the majority did, and to record individual disagreement when necessary, which none of them liked doing.

When put all together, these difficulties form a powerful cocktail. When the cocktail is added to a group setting, which in this instance is a meeting 'to protect the child' with no specified rules, it is not surprising that meetings may be unpredictable and difficult to chair.

We have already noted the mismatch for the people who chaired the conferences because of the lack of guidance as to the conventions governing the conduct of child protection conferences and therefore of chairing them, and we have hypothesised that the mismatch may arise from two sources. Firstly, that Working Together (1988) suggests registration should follow discussion which confirms abuse or neglect, thus subtly inclining the conference to consider risk in isolation rather than positives and negatives in relation to the whole. Browne and Lynch (1992) make a plea for less focus on this – 'Under the present political climate, child protection work places too much emphasis on investigation and crisis management with all the efforts directed towards proving or disproving significant harm. This is at the expense of children who primarily require help with personal and economic resources for themselves and their families.' Working Together (1991) with its shift towards partnership with parents and a more active stance towards participation with families, may enable chairs to steer a more balanced course in future, which would fit more easily with their wish to be fair.

Secondly, Working Together (1988) does not state who is accountable for the decision about registration. The chairs have had to make up their own minds as to whether they decide, or the conference decides or they take responsibility for persuading the conference to decide in line with their own view. Working Together (1991) does not clarify the matter.

Chairing well in child protection conferences

We return to the question about what is expected of the people who chair child protection conferences. Are they to run a good meeting or to get a right decision? We do not know. Both Working Together guidelines say the conference must decide about registration. To do this well, the rest of the conference needs to be conducted well. In chairing the meeting well the chances of a right decision are likely to be enhanced. In order to achieve this, chairs need to consider three things: the preparations which need to be made; the manner in which to conduct the conference; and the way the decision about registration will be made.

Preparations

- The chairs themselves spoke of the importance of setting the scene of the conference. Nearly all of them used a preamble to the conference about confidentiality. It would be easy to enlarge that preamble to assert formally, via the role of the chair, that any discriminatory remarks about race, gender, age or disability would not be acceptable in the conference. Some of the chairs already used something of the kind. It set the parameters for certain unpredictabilities.
- The use of an agenda for the conferences was another simple method of ensuring that the framework of the conference would be formally defined before the start of the meeting. Copies may be made available to all members of the conference. In some authorities the Categories of Abuse were listed on the back and the whole encased in a plastic folder and used at all conferences. An agenda provides the chairperson with a sequence of events to move through. It allows the chairperson to refer to it when members wander away from it and it provides a reason for bringing

members back to the point when extraneous information is clouding the issue.

- Chairs should not be line managers. Preserving neutrality and objectivity is essential. Part of their authority relies on their independence. It would pre-empt the chairperson having to defend social services policy or staff. The reports of the independent chairs in the study, suggest that they had an edge on the other chairs with regard to flexibility of manoeuvre about decision-making and criticism.

Manner

- The chairperson needs to be 'social work' in manner (see chapter 11) because of the nature of the subject. Child abuse and neglect cause distress, and professionals also need to be treated kindly just as families do. Recognition of distress in the reactions and over-reactions of the other professionals in the conference and acknowledgement of the tendency to act on the side of caution, rescue and control would allow for realistic consideration of alternative ideas. A 'social work' manner may facilitate an atmosphere where talking can take place. A 'social work' manner in questioning is less likely to upset people. Winning the conference over to a good group spirit would enable the process of the conference to be pushed on.

- The chairperson needs to be both 'authoritarian' and 'participatory' in method (also see chapter 10) but discriminatory as to usage. An 'authoritarian' method might be used to secure the information by keeping members to the point; it might be used to demand a high standard of reports, by focusing on the purpose of the information and explaining the need to evaluate it in relation to the safety of the child so the conference would not be deluged by it; it might be used to distinguish between fact and opinion by allowing each its proper influence; and to set goals of protection by keeping the child in the forefront of the conference members' minds. A 'participatory' method might be used to weigh up the information; to link together previous decisions; to offer alternatives; to deal with conflict; and to maintain balance by seeking positive information as well as negative information about the family.

Decision about registration

- If the chairperson were truly independent, then autocratic decision-making might be defended, in that there would be a person in charge of the meeting experienced in child abuse and neglect, and with a unique, contemporary view of what constituted child abuse and neglect locally, but we know that only one of the chairs was genuinely outside the social services hierarchy and only two others were as near independent as was possible whilst being employed and working within a Social Services Department. Even then, autocratic decision-making does not figure as a competent method of reaching a decision in the literature. Despite their best efforts the other chairs were compromised in their neutrality and objectivity and it must be concluded that their decision-making about registration was also likely to be affected similarly. So unless the well-tried and tested methods of decision-making in chapters 5 and 6 were followed, which, in the terms of this study, would be a participatory method, then the chairs would have less chance of reaching either a conference decision or a right decision. The chairs needed to expand their knowledge of leadership and decision-making skills so that they attempted both with a greater likelihood of success.

Perhaps the last word should be from the respondents about their mixed feelings regarding the chairing of child protection conferences.

> I think it was the most difficult task I was asked to perform as a manager.

> My heart-beat goes off at the start ...

> I always get stagefright beforehand.

> Someone gives you a stroke and says they like coming to your conferences.

> I do like it, especially if it comes to a good conclusion.

> The bottom line is that a child has been abused so even doing a case conference well never makes up for a child being abused.

The clearest message from the tapes is that none of the chairs found chairing easy and that even if they did it well, there remained the sadness that a child had been abused.

Appendix I

During the period of writing the thesis from which this book springs (from August 1990 to early 1993) it became increasingly apparent what a difficult task the chairing of conferences within the child protection procedures was not only because of the nature of the task itself but also because of the changing backdrop in the field of child care and particularly in child protection.

Change

Changes took place in a number of areas, not least in the name of the conferences. They used to be called 'case conferences' and became 'child protection conferences' in 1991. For the purposes of the book, in order to straddle the change in terminology, the word 'conference' has been used except where it seemed important to make the distinction. The change in name denoted a change in the nature of the conferences and this in turn required a change in chairing practice.

Working Together changes

The most immediate change resulted from the Working Together guidelines (Department of Health 1988 and 1991). Child protection has had specific guidelines since 1988, known as Working Together. They were revised in 1991 and have had a significant impact not least on chairing practice.

The responsibility for appointing people to chair the conferences has remained with the local Area Child Protection Committees. It is frequently the task of a senior manager from the Social Services Department. Although Working Together (1988) stated that the chairperson should be independent, in fact many were not. Chairs often held line management responsibility for the case being conferenced. As a result of Working Together (1991), the role of the independent chairperson has had to be addressed more seriously and changes are still occurring and still affecting the people who chair conferences.

Another major change in Working Together, directly affecting the style of chairing the conferences has been that children and parents are expected to be invited to conferences unless there are specific reasons why they should not be. Previously, they were to be invited to attend part, 'or if appropriate the whole of the case conference unless in the view of the chairman of the conference their presence would preclude a full and proper consideration of the child's interest.' (Working Together 1988) What used to be a private professional discussion, chaired in a fairly informal manner has now become a more formal meeting where family members have some rights to be present and to hear what is being said and to put their point of view. This requires a very different style of chairing. Some of the respondents at the time of interview were already chairing with parents and children present for all of the conference and some were chairing where they were present for part of the conference, but at least half were chairing where parents were not present at all. They might attend a small meeting at the end when the majority of the conference members had left. There is a different emphasis in Working Together (1991) on the process of the conference which should follow a specific pattern rather than being a general multi-disciplinary discussion.

Children Act changes

The Children Act 1989 with its focus on partnership has also been a source of change. It has not only expressed changes in thinking regarding the paramountcy of the welfare of the child, and the rights of children but also regarding parents' rights and parental responsibility, as well as safeguarding the importance of non-intervention.

Changes in public attitude

In many areas of our lives, from having access to our personal social services and health records, to reclaiming our fares if we are delayed on rail journeys, the rights of users have been promoted, at least officially. The Citizens' Charter (1992) has encapsulated the monetary tenor of the time with its emphasis on value for money and compensation for inconvenience and loss of time. It is a step in the direction of encouraging people to assert their consumer rights and citizens' rights but fails to establish the principle of rights found in the Charter of Human Rights. This Charter has not been adopted in the United Kingdom. Even the United Nations Convention on the Rights of the Child took two years before it was finally ratified by the British Government in 1991.

The rights of family members to be part of child protection procedures and in particular to attend child protection conferences, discouraged for so long in the past, should be seen in this general context of slow moves towards participation.

Changes in the criticisms in the child abuse enquiry reports

The high profile of child abuse in the 1970s and 80s as a result of the public inquiries into the deaths of a number of children escalated public anxiety and caused workers to be blamed as well as the lack of procedures. But recently the reports from Cleveland and Rochdale (1987 and 1990) pay greater attention to the decisions and plans for children made at child protection conferences and to their rights within the child protection procedures, as well as to those of their parents. The role of the chairperson in the meetings where those decisions were made was criticised and demands from the public and the Social Services Inspectorate were made for a better standard of chairing.

All these changes have had an influence on the nature of child protection conferences and therefore on the chairing of them.

Appendix II
The guided interview schedule

Most of these questions were asked in all the interviews but not necessarily in the order given below.

1. Did you have any training for chairing either inside work or outside of work or other experiences of chairing which help you?

2. Do you prepare in any way for a conference?

3. Take me through one of your conferences, please, and tell me what it was like to chair it.

    a) Which was the most difficult bit to chair?

    b) What do you do about Registration?

    c) What do you do about out of order remarks?

    d) Do you have any say about the standard of the reports?

    e) Do you have an agenda?

    f) How do you do a risk assessment?

    g) How do you get the pertinent information?

4. Do you like chairing?

5. Does your particular status in Social Services affect your chairing?

6. What do you think about the neutrality of chairs?

7. Do you have any particular theories about conferences?

8. When you chair so many conferences, how do you keep that particular child in mind?

9. What do you think about parental participation and chairing?

10. Do you think the case conference has any authority?

11. Do you think case conferences are outmoded? Do you have criticisms of them?

12. What are your views about child abuse and neglect?

13. Do you think there are case conferences and 'better' case conferences?

14. What would you say you bring to chairing from your own belief system?

15. Could you give me an analogy for a case conference?

Bibliography

Adcock, M., White, R., and Hollows, A., *Significant Harm: its management and outcome*, Croydon, Significant Publications, 1991.
Anon, *How to conduct meetings. A handbook for chairmen and all who conduct meetings*, New York, W. Foulsham and Co. Ltd., 1958.
Archard, D., *Children. Rights and Childhood*, London, Routledge, 1993.
Aries, P., *Centuries of Childhood*, Harmondsworth, Penguin, 1973.
Argyle, M., *Social Interaction*, London, Methuen, 1969.
Baglow, L.J., 'A Multidimensional Model for Treatment of Child Abuse: A Framework for Cooperation', *Child Abuse and Neglect Journal*, Vol. 14, 1990, pp. 387–395.
Baher, E., Hyman, C., Jones, C., Jones, R., Ken, A., and Mitchell, R., *At Risk: An Account of the Work of the Battered Child Research Dept.*, London, Routledge and Kegan Paul, 1976.
Bales, R.F., *Interaction Process Analysis: A Method for the Study of Small Groups*, Mass., Addison-Wesley, 1950.
Bannister, A., ed., *From Hearing to Healing: working with the Aftermath of Child Sexual Abuse*, NSPCC, Harlow, Longman, 1992.
Bannister, D. et al, *Social Casework in Marital Problems*, London, Tavistock Publications, 1955.
Bell, M. and Sinclair, I., *Parental Involvement in Initial Child Protection Conferences in Leeds: an External Evaluation*, University of York, 1993.
Benn, S.I., 'Private and Public Morality – clean living and dirty hands' in Benn, S.I, and Gans, G.F. eds, *Public and Private in Social Life*, London, Croom Helm 1983.
Berkshire study: *Parents/Carers invited to Child Protection and Case Conferences*, Chairman's Report, Bracknell 1990.
Bigelow, J., Campbell, J., Dodds, S.M., Pargetter, R., Prior, E.W. and Young, R., 'Parental Autonomy', *Journal of Applied Philosophy* pp. 183–195 Vol. 5 No. 2 1988.

Bion, W.R., *Experiences in Groups and other papers,* London, Tavistock Publications, 1961.

Bradford Study: *Parental Participation in Case Conferences,* Social Work in Partnership, University of Bradford, 1990.

Brighton Study: St Gabriel's Family Centre. Ely, D., *The Parents' Perspective on their involvement in Case Conferences,* Brighton, 1991.

Brown, A., *Groupwork,* London, Heinemann, 1979.

Browne, K.D., and Lynch, M.A., Editorial, *Journal of the British Association for the Study and Prevention of Child Abuse and Neglect,* Vol. 1., No 2., Aug. 1992, pp. 75–76.

Bryer, M., *Planning Child Care. A Guide for Team Leaders and Teams,* London, British Association of Adoption and Fostering, 1988.

Burbury, W.M., Balint, E., and Yapp, B.J., *An Introduction to Child Guidance,* London, Macmillan, 1945.

Burns, L., *Partnership with Families: a study of 65 child protection case conferences in Gloucestershire to which the Family were invited,* Gloucestershire Social Services, 1991.

Calderdale study: *Child Protection Case Conferences – Family Involvement – Research Project,* Calderdale Area Child Protection Committee, 1992.

Carver, V., ed., *Child Abuse,* Milton Keynes, Open University Press, 1978.

Charles, M. and Stevenson, O., *Multi-Disciplinary is Different!,* University of Nottingham, 1990.

Cooper, D.M. and Ball, D., *Social Work and Child Abuse,* Basingstoke, Macmillan, 1987.

Corby, B., *Child Abuse Towards a Knowledge Base,* Buckingham, Open University Press, 1993.

Corby, B., *Working with Child Abuse,* Milton Keynes, Open University Press, 1987.

Corby, B. and Mills, C., 'Child Abuse: Risks and Resources', *British Journal of Social Work,* 1986, pp. 531–542.

Creighton, S., *Trends in Child Abuse,* London, NSPCC, 1984.

Dale, P., 'Dangerous Families Revisited', *Community Care,* Nov. 14th, 1991, pp. 14–15.

Dale, P., Davies, M., Morrison, T., and Waters, J., *Dangerous Families: Assessment and Treatment of Child Abuse,* London, Tavistock Publications Ltd., 1986.

Department of Health and Social Security, LASSL(74), 13, 1974.

Department of Health *Children and Young Persons on Child Protection Registers,* Year Ending 31 March 1989 England, Government Statistical Service, London, HMSO 1990.

Department of Health *Children and Young Persons on Child Protection Registers,* Year Ending 31 March 1990 England, Government Statistical Service, London, HMSO 1991.

Department of Health, *Protecting Children: A Guide for Social Workers Undertaking a Comprehensive Assessment,* London, HMSO, 1988.

Department of Health, *The Children Act,* 1989, Chapter 41, London, HMSO, 1991.

DeMause, L. ed., *The History of Childhood,* London, Souvenir Press, 1976.

Dingwall, R., Eekalaar, J., and Murray, T., *The Protection of Children: State Intervention and Family Life,* Oxford, Basil Blackwell, 1983.

Dominelli, L. and McLeod, E., *Feminist Social Work,* Basingstoke, Macmillan, 1989.

Douglas, T., *Groups – understanding people gathered together,* London, Routledge, 1983.

Dudley study: *Involving Clients in Child Protection Review Conferences – a preliminary report,* Child Protection Team, Dudley, 1991.

Eisenhardt, K.M., 'Making Fast Strategic Decisions in High Velocity Environments', *Academy of Management Journal,* Vol. 32, No. 3, pp. 516–542.

Evans, M., *Report on the Issues for Front-line Managers in Managing Child Protection Services,* Leeds, NISW, 1990.

Everitt, A., Hardiker, P., Littlewood, J., and Mullenden, A., *Applied Research for Better Practice,* BASW, Basingstoke, Macmillan, 1992.

Filstead, W.J., 'Qualitative Methods: a Needed Perspective in Evaluation Research' in Cook, T.D., and Reichardt, C.S. (eds) *Qualitative and Quantitative Methods in Evaluation Research,* London, Sage, 1979.

Frost, M. and Stein, M., *Politics of Child Welfare,* Hemel Hempstead, Harvester Wheatsheaf, 1989.

Gathorne-Hardy, J., *The Rise and Fall of the British Nanny,* London, Arrow Books, 1972.

Gibb, C., 'Groups stay poles apart', *Social Work Today,* Aug. 31st, 1989.

Gibbons, J., *Purposes and Organisation of Preventative Work with Families: The Two-Area Study,* London, HMSO, 1989.

Gillick v. West Norfolk and Wisbech Area Health Authority 1985.

Gilmour, A., *Innocent Victims. The Question of Child Abuse,* London, Michael Joseph, 1988.

Greenland, C., *Preventing Child Abuse and Neglect Deaths,* London, Tavistock Publications, 1987.

Hallett, C., and Birchall, E., *Co-ordination in Child Protection – a review of the literature,* London, HMSO, 1992.

Hallett, C., and Stevenson, O., *Child Abuse: Aspects of Inter-professional Co-operation,* London, Allen and Unwin, 1980.

Hardyment, C., *Dream Babies,* London, Jonathan Cape, 1983.

Higginson, S., 'Forty Case Conferences – Distorted Evidence', *Community Care,* May 17th, 1991, pp. 23–25.

Hirschhorn, L., *The Workplace Within: the Psychodynamics of the Workplace,* Massachusetts USA, Murray Printing Co., 1988.

Hutchinson, R., 'The Effect of Enquiries into Cases of Child Abuse upon the Social Work Profession', *British Journal of Criminology,* 1986.

Irvine, E., 'Children at Risk' in Younghusband, E, ed., *Social Work with Families,* NISW, Allen and Unwin, 1965.

Janis, I.L., and Mann, L., *Decision-making,* New York, The Free Press, 1977.

Kellmer Pringle, M.L. (ed.) *Caring for Children,* London, Longman, 1969.

Kelly, L., *Surviving Sexual Violence,* Polity Press, Cambridge, 1988.

Kendrick, A. and Mapstone, E., 'The Chairperson and Child Care Reviews in Scotland. Implications for the role of reviews in the decision-making process', *British Journal of Social Work* 17, 1989, pp. 277–289.

Kevill-Davies, S., *Yesterdays Children – the Antiques and History of Child Care,* Suffolk Antique Collectors' Club, 1991.

Lynch, M. and Roberts, J., *Consequences of Child Abuse,* New York, Academic Press, 1982.

Lynch, M. and Roberts, J., 'Predicting Child Abuse: signs of bonding failure in the Maternity Hospital', *British Medical Journal,* Vol. 1, 1977, pp. 624–36.

Luckham, S. and Marchant, A., *A Study of Parental and Child Participation in Child Protection Case Conferences in Mid-Essex,* Essex County Council, 1991.

McGrew, A.G. and Wilson, M.J., *Decision-making,* Milton Keynes, Open University, 1984.

Mead, M. and Byers, P., *The Small Conference – an innovation in Communication,* Paris, Montin and Co., 1968.

Menzies, I.E.P., *The Functioning of Social Systems as a Defence against Anxiety,* Tavistock Institute of Human Relations, London, 1961.

Mintzberg and Waters, Pettigrew and Butler, 'Studying, deciding: an exchange of views', *Organisational Studies Journal* 11, Issue 1, p. 1–16.

Mitchell, G., *Workshop on Child Protection,* Liverpool Polytechnic, 1989.

Moore, J., *The ABC of Child Abuse Work,* Aldershot, Gower, 1985.

Moore, J., *The ABC of Child Protection,* Aldershot, Ashgate, 1992.

Morgan, H., *What 10 Social Workers bring to the decision-making process in Child Protection Work,* MSW thesis, University of East Anglia, unpublished, 1989.

North Yorkshire study: *Family Participation in Child Protection Case Conferences,* N. Yorkshire Area Child Protection Committee, 1991.

Owen, H. and Pritchard, J., eds, *Good Practice in Child Protection,* London, Jessica Kingsley Publishers Ltd, 1993.

Owen, M., *Voluntary Care in Difficult Cases,* Social Work Monographs, University of East Anglia, 1991.

Packman, J., Randall, T., and Jacques, N., *Who Needs Care?,* Oxford, Basil Blackwell, 1986.

Page, E., 'Parental Rights', *Journal of Applied Philosophy,* pp. 187–203 Vol. 1 No. 2 1984.

Parry, G. and Morris, P., 'When is a decision not a decision?' in McGrew, A.G and Wilson, M.J., *Decision-making,* Milton Keynes, Open University, 1982.

Parton, C. and Parton, N., 'Women, the family and child protection', *Journal of Critical Social Policy* 8, 3, pp. 38–49.
Parton, N., *The Politics of Child Abuse,* London, Macmillan, 1985.
Pemberton, M., *Effective Meetings,* Communication Skills Guides, Windsor, The Industrial Social Press, 1982.
Phillips, J., and Evans, M., *Participating Parents,* Bradford, ADB Publications. 1986.
Phillips, G.M., Pedersen, D.J. and Wood, J.T, *A Practical Guide to participation and leadership,* Boston USA, Houghton Mifflin Co.
Pollock, L. A., *Forgotten Children. Parent-child relationships from 1500 to 1900,* Cambridge, Cambridge University Press, 1983.
Pottage, D. and Evans, M., *Workbased Stress: Prescription is not the cure,* London, NISW, 1992.
Reder, P., Duncan, S. and Gray, M., *Beyond Blame. Child Abuse Tragedies Revisited,* London, Routledge, 1993.
Report of Committee of Inquiry into the Care and Supervision Provided in Relation to Maria Colwell, London HMSO, 1974.
Report of the Committee of Inquiry into Provisions and Co-ordination of Services to the Family of John George Auckland, London, HMSO, 1975.
Report of an independent inquiry on Maria Mehmedagi, London Borough of Southwark, 1981.
Report of the Inquiry into Child Abuse in Cleveland, Cmnd 412, London, HMSO, 1987.
Report of the Inquiry into the Removal of Children from Orkney in February 1991, Edinburgh, HMSO.
Report on Kimberley Carlile. A Child in Mind: protection of children in a responsible society, Borough of Greenwich, London, 1987.
Report of a panel appointed by the Essex Area Review Committee on Malcolm Page, Essex County Council and Essex Health Authority, 1981.
Report of the panel of inquiry into the circumstances surrounding the death of Jasmine Beckford: A Child in Trust, London, Borough of Brent, 1985.
Richmond, M. and Rapoport, L., 'Towards a definition of Social Casework' *Social Work Quarterly Review of Family Casework,* Vol. 11, No. 2, April 1954, pp. 910–911, Family Welfare Association.
Roche, J., 'Children's Rights and the Welfare of the Child' in *Child Abuse and Neglect – Facing the Challenge,* Stainton-Rogers, W., Hevey, D. and Ash, E. Open University and Batsford Ltd, London, 1989.
Sheffield Study: Woodhill, R. and Ashworth, P., *Parental Participation in Case Conferences,* Sheffield University, 1989.
Shemmings, D., *Family Participation in Child Protection Conferences: 2. Report of a pilot project in Lewisham Social Services,* Norwich, UEA, 1991.
Sinclair, R., *Decision-making in Statutory Reviews on Children in Care,* Aldershot, Gower, 1984.

Stainton-Rogers, R. and W., *Stories of Childhood – shifting agendas of child concern,* Hemel Hempstead, Harvester Wheatsheaf, 1992.

Strauss, B.W. and Strauss, F., *New Ways to better meetings,* London, Tavistock Publications Ltd., 1964.

Social Services Inspectorate Reports:
 Child Protection Services in Manchester, 1990;
 Child Protection Services in Rochdale, 1991.

Thoburn, J., *Captive Clients: Social Work with Families of Children Home on Trial,* London, Routledge and Kegan Paul, 1980.

Thoburn, J., *Participation in Practice – involving Families in Child Protection,* Norwich, UEA, 1992.

Thoburn, J., Lewis, A., Shemmings, D., *Family Involvement in Child Protection Conferences,* Discussion paper 1, Norwich, UEA, 1992.

Thoburn, J., Lewis, A., Shemmings, D., *Family Participation in Child Protection: Report for the Department of Health,* Norwich, UEA, forthcoming.

Thoburn, J., and Shemmings, D., *Parental Participation in Child Protection Conferences: Report of a pilot project in Hackney SSD,* Norwich, UEA, 1990.

Thompson, S. and Kahn, T.H., *The Group Process as a Helping Technique,* Oxford, Pergamon Press, 1970.

United Nations Convention on the Rights of the Child, adopted by the United Nations General Assembly November 1989; ratified by the British Government December 1991.

Wade, D., *Behind the Speakers Chair,* Leeds and London, Austwick, 1978.

Waldron, J., *Theories of Rights,* Oxford University Press, 1984.

Wallach, M.A., Kogan, N., Benn, D.J., 'Diffusion of responsibility and level of risk-taking in Groups', *Journal of Abnormal and Social Psychology,* Vol. 68, No. 3, pp. 263–274, 1964.

Whale, M., 'Problem Families – the case for social casework', *Social Work Quarterly Review of Family Casework,* SW Vol. 11, No. 1, Jan. 1954, Family Welfare Association.

White Franklin, A. ed., *Papers presented by the Tunbridge Wells Study Group on Non-Accidental Injury to Children,* London, Churchill Livingston, 1975.

Williams, A.P. O., 'Systematic Decision-making in the Child Care Service. Attitudes reflected in 3 research seminars', *Social Work, The British Quarterly Journal,* Vol. 25, No. 2, 1968.

Wilkins, L.T., *Confidence and Competence in Decision-making,* London, Tavistock Publications Ltd., 1964.

Wiltshire study: Lonsdale, G., *A Survey of Parental Participation at Initial Child Protection Case Conferences,* 1991.

Working Together under the Children Act 1989: A Guide to Arrangements for inter-agency co-operation for the protection of children from abuse, London, HMSO, 1988 and 1991.

Younghusband, E., *Social Work with Families,* NISW, Allen and Unwin, 1965.